Elisha A. Hoffman

Spiritual Songs for Gospel Meetings and the Sunday School

Elisha A. Hoffman

Spiritual Songs for Gospel Meetings and the Sunday School

ISBN/EAN: 9783337430467

Printed in Europe, USA, Canada, Australia, Japan

Cover: Foto ©Thomas Meinert / pixelio.de

More available books at **www.hansebooks.com**

SPIRITUAL SONGS

FOR

GOSPEL MEETINGS

AND THE

SUNDAY SCHOOL,

BY

Rev. ELISHA A. HOFFMAN,

AND J. H. TENNEY.

PUBLISHED BY
SAMUEL BARKER,
No. 74 Superior Street, Cleveland, O.

TO JESUS,

OUR PRECIOUS REDEEMER, who is the theme of our song, and to the **FRIENDS OF THE MASTER**, who love his appearing, and delight to sing his praise, these

"Spiritual Songs"

Are consecrated, in the hope that the Saviour may be glorified in them, that his people may be comforted, blessed, quickened and strengthened, and that some erring souls may be won to the Cross thereby.

THE BOOK IS ADAPTED FOR

Gospel Meetings,   *Sunday Schools,*   *Prayer Meetings,*
Conventions,   *Camp Meetings,*   *Institutes,*
Y. M. C. A. Meetings,   *Assemblies,*
Mission Churches, &c.,

And wherever song is used as an element of worship. In humble consecration, we lay the book at the feet of the blessed Master.

> "WITH grateful hearts, O Lord, we bring
> These psalms, and hymns, and songs to thee;
> Content to serve in anything,
> So we may but thy servants be.
>
> Accept and bless the songs we sing,
> And tune our souls to loftier strains,
> So we may join the notes that ring
> Triumphant o'er the heavenly plains."—H. B. H.

"Unto him who loved us, and washed us from our sins in his own blood, and hath made us kings and priests unto God and his Father; to him be glory and dominion for ever and ever, Amen."

ELISHA A. HOFFMAN,
J. H. TENNEY.

SELECTIONS FOR EXAMINATION.

NEW SONGS—7, 9, 15, 19, 22, 29, 31, 32, 45, 52, 58, 70, 71, 77, 80.
NEW SONGS BY P. P. BLISS—3, 4, 17, 33, 66, 69.
SONGS ALREADY POPULAR—5, 6, 8, 11, 14, 25, 34, 38, 43, 49, 50, 54, 59, 61, 64, 67, 68, 70, 78, 81.

Entered according to Act of Congress, in the year 1878, by Elisha A. Hoffman, in the Office of the Librarian of Congress, at Washington.

SPIRITUAL SONGS.

The Shadow Of The Cross.

3. A stranger here, I pitch my tent
   Beneath this spreading tree:
   Here shall my pilgrim life be spent;
   No home like this for me!

4. For burden'd ones a resting place
   Beside that cross I see;
   I here cast off my weariness;
   No rest like this for me!

This Is Why I Love My Jesus.

Rev. Elisha A. Hoffman.

2. Would you know why I love Jesus?
   Why he is so dear to me?
   'Tis because the blood of Jesus
   Fully saves and cleanses me.

3. Would you know why I love Jesus?
   Why he is so dear to me?
   'Tis because, amid temptation,
   He supports and strengthens me.

4. Would you know why I love Jesus?
   Why he is so dear to me?
   'Tis because in every conflict
   Jesus gives me victory.

5. Would you know why I love Jesus?
   Why he is so dear to me?
   'Tis because, my friend and Savior
   He will ever, ever be.

Why Don't You Come To Jesus?

C. R. Dunbar, by per.

1. Je-sus now is my sal-va-tion, He has saved me from all sin;
Thro' his blood I have re-demp-tion,
2. By his royal pro-cla-ma-tion, Sin's do-min-ion now is o'er,
And in conscious full sal-va-tion
3. Oh, the love of my Re-deem-er! Oh, the wonders of his grace!
I will praise his name forever,

And I rest complete in him.
I may sing forever-more.
And rejoice before his face.

Semi-Chorus.
O the joy of full sal-va-tion!
Spread the news to every na-tion:

How it thrills my inmost soul!
Je-sus blood has made me whole.

Full Chorus. p   m   f
Why don't you come to Je-sus? why don't you come to Je-sus? why don't you come to Je-sus and be saved? . . . . . saved?

The Savior's Call.

Words and Music by CHAS. H. GABRIEL.

1. At the door I'm knocking, knocking, Will you rise and let me in?
2. At the door I'm knocking, knocking, But the door is hard to move;
3. At the door I'm knocking, knocking, But I'm wait-ing all in vain;
4. At the door I'm knocking, knocking, Must I, must I now de-part?

Chorus.

I am waiting, on-ly waiting To forgive your every sin.
For the rus-ty hinges give not, While I wait in hope and love. 'Tis the
Closely is the i-vy clinging; Will the door unbarred remain?
For so much, so much I love you, And I want your weary heart.

voice of Je-sus call-ing, While his heart in pit-y bleeds; Will you

o-pen wide the door way, While so ten-der-ly he pleads?

Evergreen Plain.

Rev. I. BALTZELL, by per.

1. Shall we meet beyond the river, In that clime where angels dwell? Shall we meet where friendship never, Saddest tales of sorrow tell?
2. Shall we meet where flow'rs are blooming, Ever fadeless, ever fair; Where the light of day illumines, Lives of those who enter there?
3. Shall we meet our loved companions, On that brighter, fairer shore? When this life's great work is ended, Shall we meet to part no more?
4. Yes! we'll meet beyond the river, Where our joys shall never die, We shall meet our lov'd and lost ones, In that happy by and by.

Chorus.

Shall we meet,......... shall we meet,...... Shall we meet on the evergreen
Shall we meet, shall we meet,

Rit.

plain? Shall we meet and know each other ever, Shall we never part again?

Are You Washed In The Blood?

15

E. A. H. E. A. H.

1. Have you been to Jesus for the cleansing pow'r? Are you washed in the blood of the Lamb? Are you fully trusting in his grace this hour? Are you washed in the blood of the Lamb?
2. Are you walking daily by the Savior's side? Are you washed in the blood of the Lamb? Do you rest each moment in the Crucified? Are you washed in the blood of the Lamb?
3. When the Bridegroom cometh, will your robes be white, Pure and white in the blood of the Lamb? Will your soul be ready for the mansions bright, And be washed in the blood of the Lamb?
4. Lay aside the garments that are stained with sin, And be washed in the blood of the Lamb; There's a fountain flowing for the soul unclean, O be washed in the blood of the Lamb!

Chorus.

Are you washed in the blood, In the soul-cleansing blood of the Lamb? Are your garments spotless? Are they white as snow? Are you washed in the blood of the Lamb?

God Is Coming.

Mrs. Sue M. O. Hoffman.

1. God is coming! God is coming! shout aloud the glad re-frain;
2. God is coming! God is coming! roll the notes of joy on high;
3. God is coming! God is coming! and the hosts of sin are strong;
4. God is coming! God is coming! O lift up your hearts and pray!

Send the cry from town and cit-y to the vil-lage, ham let, plain;
Ev-ery blood-bought son of Je-sus, ral - ly to your lead-er's cry!
We will meet them bravely, bold-ly, and the fight will not be long.
In the fight 'twixt light and darkness he will need strong arms to-day.

D.S. *Every man be up on du-ty, For Je-hov-ah comes this way.*

God is com-ing! hear the an - gels shout the tidings from above;
God is com-ing! God is com-ing! rub your rus-ty ar-mor bright,
God is com-ing! and be-fore him powers of darkness must give way;
God is com-ing! fal-ter nev - er—when the conflict here is done

He will de-luge our whole country with his ti-dal wave of love.
Gird your sword and shield about you, and be read-y for the fight.
God is com-ing! by his strong arm we shall gain the vic-to-ry;
You shall wear a crown of glo-ry in the kingdom of his Son.

Chorus.

God is com-ing! pass the watchword all a-long the line to-day!

42. Have You Not A Word For Jesus?

From "Songs of Gratitude," by per. J. H. FILLMORE.

1. Have you not a word for Jesus? Will the world his praise proclaim?
Who shall speak if ye are si-lent, Ye who know and love his name?
Ye whom he hath called and chosen His own witnesses to be,
Will you tell your gracious Master, "Lord, we cannot speak for thee?"

2. He has spoken words of bless-ing, Par-don, peace and love to you,
Glo-rious hope and gracious comfort, Strong and tender, sweet and true?
Does he hear you telling others Something of his love untold,
O-verflow-ings of thanksgiv-ing For his mer-cies man-i-fold?

3. Have you not a word for Jesus? Some, perchance, while ye are dumb,
Wait and weary for your message, Hoping you will bid them come;
Never telling hidden sorrows, Ling'ring just outside the door,
Longing for your hand to lead them Into rest forevermore.

4. Yours may be the joy and honor Some poor ransomed souls to bring,
Jewels for the coronation Of your coming Lord and King;
Will you cast away the gladness, Thus your Master's joy to share,
All because a word for Jesus Seems too much for you to dare?

The Sun Of Righteousness.

1. As the rising sun disperses
All the gloomy shades of night,
So the coming of the Savior
Turns our darkness into light.

Refrain.
Sun of Glory! shine forever,
In this lowly heart of mine;
Take away all sin and darkness;
Fill me with thy love divine.

2. Light and life, and joy and beauty,
Everywhere his coming brings;
Weep no longer, trembling mourner,
There is healing in his wings.

3. Christ has come! My soul, receive him,
Why one moment more delay?
He is ready, he is waiting
All thy sins to wash away.

MRS. MARY F. MARSH.

As sung by Mr. SANKEY and Boston Tabernacle Choir.

My Spirit is Free. 43

W. A. S.
Rev. W. A. SPENCER, by per.

1. I fol-low the foot-steps of Je-sus, my Lord, His Spir-it doth lead me a-long; I walk in the path-way made plain by His word, And He fills all my soul with this song.
2. A lep-er he found me, pol-lut-ed by sin, From which he a-lone can set free; He spake in His mer-cy, "I will, be thou clean," And He in-stant-ly pu-ri-fied me.
3. A cap-tive in woe to my pris-on of night The Mas-ter hath o-pen'd the door; Shout a-loud of deliv'rance, ye an-gels of light, Praise His name, oh my soul, ev-er-more.
4. Pro-claim it, 'tis done, full sal-va-tion is wrought For sin-ners from sor-row and woe; Sing a-loud of His grace who my par-don has bought, "For His blood washes whit-er than snow."

Chorus.

Glo-ry to God! my spir-it is free, Glo-ry to God, He pu-ri-fies me! I'm walking the thorn-path, but joyful I'll be While following Je-sus my Lord.

There Is Joy In Heaven.

Rev. H. B. Hartzler.   J. H. T.

1. There is joy in heaven, where the angels dwell, And the gladsome notes of rejoicing swell,
2. There is joy in heaven, when the lost is found, And the golden streets with the news resound,
3. There is joy in heaven, that begins below, Where the tears of grief and repentance flow;

When the tidings come from the world below, That a soul is saved from eternal woe.
Till the tide of song like an ocean rolls Unto Him who died for the love of souls.
And the saints of God with the angels share In the praise that rings like an anthem there.

Chorus.

Beautiful song! Beautiful song! Beautiful song! Beautiful song of joy!
Beautiful song! Beautiful song! Beautiful song! Beautiful song of joy!

Ev'ry harp is at·tuned un-to the sound, And the angels re-joice that the lost is found, Beautiful song! Beautiful song of joy!

Song of joy, Beau-ti-ful song, hap-py song of joy!

52. Jesus Is Passing This Way.

E. A. H.
J. H. T.

1. Is there a sin-ner a-wait-ing Mer-cy and pardon to-day?
2. Brother, the Master is wait-ing, Waiting to free-ly for-give;
3. Yes, he is coming to bless you While in contrition you bow;

Welcome the news that we bring him: "Jesus is passing this way!"
Why not this moment accept him, Trust in his grace and live?
Coming from sin to re-deem you, Read-y to save you now;

Coming in love and in mer-cy, Pardon and peace to be-stow,
He is so tender and pre-cious, He is so near you to-day;
Can you re-fuse the sal-va-tion Je-sus is of-fer-ing here?

Coming to save the poor sin-ner From his heart-anguish and woe.
O-pen your heart to receive him, While he is passing this way.
O-pen your heart to ad-mit him, While he is coming so near.

Chorus.

Je-sus is passing this way...... To-day,......... to-day,
Jesus is passing this way, To-day, is passing to-day!

My Anchor Is Holding.

Mrs. E. W. Chapman. J. H. Tenney, by per.

"Which hope we have as an anchor of the soul." Heb. 6, 19.

1. Sweet Hope, the anchor of my soul, Enters within the vail; Rests in the Saviour's dying love; Fears not the wildest gale.
2. My life's frail bark is often tossed, High on the mountain waves Steadfast and sure my anchor holds, Firm on the Rock that saves.
3. Fair Heaven's dome is just in view, Beautiful, golden land! Soon I shall reach its gate of pearl, Walk on its shining strand.

CHORUS.

My anchor is holding, is holding, Within the vail; My anchor is holding, is holding, It will not fail.

When We All Get Home.—CONCLUDED.

glo-ry we shall see, When we all get home, ov-er there, ov-er there.

Nearer The Cross.

Mrs. VALENSTYNE.   Mrs. J. F. KNAPP, by per.

1. Nearer the cross, my heart can say, I'm coming near-er;
Nearer the cross from day to day, I'm coming .... near-er.

{ Nearer the cross where Je-sus died,
Nearer the foun-tain's crimson tide, } Near-er my Sav-ior's wound-ed side, I'm com-ing near-er, I'm com-ing near-er.

2. Nearer the Christian's mercy-seat,
Feasting my soul on manna sweet,
Stronger in faith, more clear I see,
Jesus who gave himself for me,
Nearer to him I still would be,
  Still coming nearer.

3. Nearer in prayer my hope aspires,
Deeper the love my soul desires,
Nearer the end of toil and care,
Nearer the joy I long to share,
Nearer the crown I soon shall wear,
  I'm coming nearer.

2. 'Tis grace! 'tis grace! 'tis wonderful grace!
   Which saves the soul from sin;
   The power of rising evil slays,
   And reigns supreme within.

3. 'Tis grace! 'tis grace! 'tis wonderful grace!
   Its streams are full and free;
   Are flowing now for all the race,
   They even flow to me.

There's Light Over There.—CONCLUDED.

Come To Jesus.

E. R. LATTA.   J. H. T.

1. Come to Je-sus! he will save you, Tho' your sins as crimson glow;
   If you give your hearts to Je - sus, He will make them white as snow.
2. Come to Je-sus! do not tar - ry; En-ter in at mercy's gate;
   O de - lay not till the mor - row, Lest thy coming be too late.
3. Come to Je-sus, dy-ing sin - ner! Oth-er Sav-ior there is none;
   He will share with you his glory, When your pilgrimage is done.

Chorus.

Come to Je - sus! Come to Je - sus!
Come, come to-day! Come, come to-day!

Come to Jesus! come to-day,
Come to Jesus! come, yes, come, come to-day!
Come to Jesus! come, come to-day!

Deliverance Will Come.

Arr. by Rev. W. McDonald, by per.

1. I saw a way-worn traveler in tattered garments clad, And struggling up the mountain, It seemed that he was sad; His back was laden heavy, His strength was almost gone, Yet he shouted as he journeyed, Deliverance will come. Cho.—Then palms of victory, Crowns of glory, Palms of victory, I shall wear.

2. I saw him in the evening,
The sun was bending low,
Had overtopped the mountain
And reached the vale below:
He saw the golden city,
His everlasting home,
And shouted loud hosanna!
Deliverance will come.

3. While gazing on that city
Just o'er the narrow flood,
A band of holy angels
Came from the throne of God;
They bore him on their pinions,
Safe o'er the dashing foam,
And joined him in his triumph,—
Deliverance has come.

My Father's House.

Ellen M. H. Gates. Furnished by Mr. Sankey. W. O. Perkins, by per.

1. I am far away from my Father's house, And the years increase, The lights are dim in the banquet halls, The wreaths are withering

My Father's House.—CONCLUDED.

2. I have sought the best that the world could give,
As an idle guest,
My Father's house with its mansions fair,
Is the place for me, and my heart is there,
For my home is best.

3. O the doubts and fears of the changeful years;
They have vex'd my soul!
But safe forever and white and grand,
My Father's house like a rock will stand,
While the ages roll.

No Time for Jesus.

CHAS. H. GABRIEL.   J. H. T.

1. No time to give to Je - sus! O soul, what dost thou say?
Wilt thou not, for thy Sav-ior Give . . . of thy time to-day? His pre-cious life a ran-som For thee he freely gave; He left his throne in glo - ry Thy sin - ful soul to save.

2. No time to give to Jesus!
O thankless soul! why not?
Remember, by his mercy,
Thy precious soul was bought;
Canst thou not, from thy moments,
Find time to give to prayer?
In faithful vineyard-labor
Some moments for him spare?—Cho.

No, Not Despairingly. CONCLUDED.

still my plea. Je - sus hath died for me, Je - sus hath died.

2. Lord, I confess to thee
  Sadly my sin;
  Now, tell I all to thee,
  All I have been;
  Purge thou my sin away,
  Wash thou my soul this day,
  Take thou my sin away;
  Lord, make me clean.

3. Faithful and just art thou,
  Forgiving all;
  Loving and kind art thou,
  When sorrows call;
  Lord, let the cleansing blood,
  Let the dear healing flood,
  Blood of the Lamb of God,
  Pass o'er my soul.

I Shall Be Satisfied.

DR. H. BONAR. REV. T. C. NEAL.
Moderato.

1. When I shall wake in that fair morn of morns, Af-ter whose dawn-ing
2. When I shall see thy glo-ry face to face, When in thine arms thou
3. When I shall meet with those that I have loved, Clasp in my ea-ger
4. When I shall gaze up-on the face of him Who for me died, with

never night returns, And with whose glory day eternal burns, I shall be sat-is-fied.
wilt thy child embrace, When thou shalt open all thy stores of grace, I shall be satisfied.
arms the long removed, And find how faithful thou to me hast proved, I shall be satisfied.
eye no longer dim, And praise him with the everlasting hymn, I shall be sat-is-fied.

Chorus.   rit.

I shall be sat-is-fied, I shall be sat-is-fied, I shall be sat-is-fied, By and by.

From "Jasper and Gold," by per.

Room for Jesus.

Rev. T. J. SHELTON.   J. H. T.

1. Je - sus, I have room for thee, In my hum - ble dwell - ing;
2. Room with-in my heart for thee, Life's e - ter - nal foun - tain!
3. Room with-in my heart for thee, Suff'-rer in the gar - den!

Come to me a wel-come guest, All my sins ex - pell - ing.
Room for Christ who bore the cross Up to Calv' - ry's moun - tain.
If thou bring thy peace to me, If thou seal my par - don.

D.S. Come and seal me with thy love, And be - stow thy fa - vor.

Chorus.

Room for thee, room for thee, Pre - cious Lord and Sav - ior!

The Better Day Coming On.

M. L. ROSSVALLEY, by per.

1. My Je - sus, I love thee! I know thou art mine,
    My gra - cious Re - deem - er, my Sav - ior art thou,

Chorus.—There's a bet - ter day, there's a crowning day, There's a bet - ter day com-ing
    Coming on, Coming on, Coming on, com-ing

For thee all the pleas - ures of sin I re - sign;
If ev - er I lov'd thee, my Je - sus, 'tis now.

on, There's a bet-ter day, there's a crowning day, There's a better day coming on.
on, There's a bet-ter day, there's a crowning day, There's a better day coming on.

2. I love thee because thou hast first loved me,
And purchased my pardon, being nailed to the tree;
I love thee for wearing the thorns on thy brow,
If ever I loved thee, my Jesus, 'tis now.—

3. In mansions of glory, or heavenly delight,
I'll ever adore thee in regions of light;
And sing with a glittering crown on my brow,
If ever I loved thee, my Jesus, 'tis now.

1

Just as I am, without one plea,
  But that thy blood was shed for me,
And that thou bid'st me come to thee,
O Lamb of God! I come, I come!

Just as I am, and waiting not
To rid my soul of one dark blot,
To thee, whose blood can cleanse each spot
  O Lamb of God! I come, I come!

Just as I am; thou wilt receive,
Wilt welcome, pardon, cleanse, relieve;
Because thy promise I believe,
  O Lamb of God! I come, I come!

2.

Oh, take my fevered hands in thine,
  And keep me Master, nearer thee,
Walking above the things of time,
  In closest fellowship with thee.

Calm in thy secret presence, Lord,
  I rest this weary soul of mine,
Feed on the fullness of thy word,
  And die to all the things of time;

Such be my path while dwelling here,
  One long, close, upward path with thee;
Until, past every doubt and fear,
  Thy face in light above I see.

3.

O God, forgive the years and years
  Of worldly pride and hopes and fears;
Forgive, and blot them from thy book,
  The sins on which I mourn to look.

Forgive the lack of service done
For thee, thro' life, from life begun;
Forgive the vain desire to be
All else but that desired by thee.

Forgive the love of human praise,
The first false step in crooked ways,
The voice of evil and the night,
The heart close shut against the light.

Forgive the love that could endure
No cost to bless the sad and poor;
Forgive, and give me grace to see
The life laid down in love for me.

4.

When I survey the wondrous cross
  On which the Prince of glory died,
My richest gain I count but loss,
  And pour contempt on all my pride.

See, from his head, his hands, his feet,
  Sorrow and love flow mingled down;
Did e'er such love and sorrow meet,
  Or thorns compose so rich a crown?

Were the whole realm of nature mine,
  That were a present far too small;
Love so amazing, so divine,
  Demands my soul, my life, my all!

5.

Lord, I am thine, entirely thine,
  Purchased and saved by blood divine;
With full consent thine I would be,
And own thy sov'reign right in me.

Thine would I live, thine would I die;
Be thine through all eternity;
The vow is past, beyond repeal,
And now I set the solemn seal.

Here, at that cross where flows the blood
That bought my guilty soul for God,
Thee, my new Master, now I call,
And consecrate to thee my all.

6.

Come, Saviour, Jesus, from above,
  Assist me with thy heavenly grace;
Empty my heart of earthly love,
  And for thyself prepare the place.

O let thy sacred presence fill,
  And set my longing spirit free;
Which pants to have no other will,
  But day and night to feast on thee.

Henceforth may no profane delight
  Divide this consecrated soul;
Possess it thou, who hast the right,
  As Lord and Master of the whole.

7.

With tearful eyes I look around,
  Life seems a dark and stormy sea;
Yet 'midst the gloom I hear a sound,
  A heavenly whisper, "Come to me."

It tells me of a place of rest—
  It tells me where my soul may flee;
Oh! to the weary, faint, oppressed,
  How sweet the bidding, "Come to me."

O voice of mercy! voice of love!
  In conflict, grief and agony,
Support me, cheer me from above!
  And gently whisper, "Come to me."

8.

Show pity, Lord, O Lord forgive!
  Let a repenting rebel live;
Are not thy mercies large and free?
May not a sinner trust in thee?

My crimes are great, but can't surpass
The power and glory of thy grace;
Great God, thy nature hath no bound,
So let thy Pardoning love be found.

Oh wash my soul from every sin,
And make my guilty conscience clean;
Here on my heart the burden lies,
And past offenses pain mine eyes.

Yet save a trembling sinner, Lord,
Whose hope still hov'ring round thy word,
Would light on some sweet promise there,
Some sure support against despair.

9.

O that my load of sin were gone;
  O that I could at last submit
At Jesus' feet to lay it down—
  To lay my soul at Jesus' feet.

Rest for my soul I long to find;
  Saviour of all, if mine thou art,
Give me thy meek and lowly mind,
  And stamp thine image on my heart.

Break off the yoke of inbred sin,
  And fully set my spirit free;
I cannot rest till pure within,—
  Till I am wholly lost in thee.

1.

O, BEULAH Land! Fair Beulah Land!
  Upon the shore of earth I stand,
And look across the narrow sea
That seperates yon Heaven from me.

O, Beulah Land, bright Beulah Land!
I feel my raptured soul expand
As I, with eager faith, behold
Yon walls of jasper, gates of gold.

O, Beulah Land! sweet vale of peace,
Whose very air is full of bliss,
I linger in thy bowers of prayer,
The fragrance of God's love is there.

2.

I THIRST, thou wounded Lamb of God,
  To wash me in thy cleansing blood:
To dwell within thy wounds: then pain
Is sweet, and life or death is gain.

Take my poor heart, and let it be
Forever closed to all but thee:
Seal thou my breast, and let me wear
That pledge of love forever there.

3.

FROM every stormy wind that blows,
  From every swelling tide of woes,
There is a calm, a sure retreat;
'Tis found beneath the mercy-seat.

There is a place where Jesus sheds
The oil of gladness on our heads—
A place than all besides more sweet;
It is the blood bought mercy-seat.

There, there on eagle wings we soar,
And sin and sense molest no more;
And heaven comes down our souls to greet,
And glory crowns the mercy-seat.

4.

JESUS! and shall it ever be,
  A mortal man ashamed of thee!
Ashamed of thee, whom angels praise,
Whose glories shine through endless days!

Ashamed of Jesus, that dear friend,
On whom my hopes of heaven depend!
No, when I blush, be this my shame,
That I no more revere his name.

Ashamed of Jesus! yes, I may,
When I've no guilt to wash away,
No tears to wipe, no good to crave,
No fears to quell, no soul to save.

5.

SAY, sinner! hath a voice within,
  Oft whispered to thy secret soul,
Urged thee to leave the ways of sin,
And yield thy heart to God's control?

Sinner, it was a heavenly voice,—
It was the Spirit's gracious call;
It bade thee make the better choice,
And haste to seek in Christ thine all.

Spurn not the call to life and light;
Regard, in time, the warning kind;
That call thou mayst not always slight,
And yet the gate of mercy find.

6.

JESUS, a word, a look from thee,
  Can turn my heart, and make it clean,
Purge out the inbred leprosy,
And save me from my bosom sin.

My heart, which now to thee I raise,
I know thou canst this moment cleanse,
The deepest stains of sin efface,
And drive the evil spirit hence.

Be it according to thy word;
Accomplish now thy work in me,
And let my soul, to health restored,
Devote its deathless powers to thee.

7.

O LORD, thy sovereign aid impart,
  And guard the gift thyself hast given:
My portion thou, my treasure art,
My life, and happiness, and heaven.

Would aught on earth my wishes share?
Though dear as life the idol be,
The idol from my breast I'll tear,
Resolved to seek my all in thee.

Whate'er I fondly counted mine,
To thee, my Lord, I here restore;
Gladly I all to thee resign;
Give me thyself, I ask no more.

8.

COME, Holy Spirit! calm my mind,
  And fit me to approach my God;
Remove each vain, each worldly thought,
And lead me to thy blest abode.

Hast thou imparted to my soul
A living spark of holy fire?
Oh! kindle now the sacred flame;
Make me to burn with pure desire.

A brighter faith and hope impart,
And let me now my Saviour see;
Oh! soothe and cheer my burdened heart,
And bid my spirit rest in thee.

9.

AWAKE, my soul, in joyful lays,
  And sing thy great Redeemer's praise;
He justly claims a song from thee,
His loving kindness oh, how free!

He saw me ruined in the fall,
Yet loved me notwithstanding all;
He saved me from my lost estate,
His loving kindness, oh, how great!

Often I feel my sinful heart
Prone from my Saviour to depart;
But, though I oft have him forgot,
His loving kindness changes not.

Soon shall I pass the gloomy vale,
Soon all my mortal powers must fail;
Oh, may my last expiring breath
His loving kindness sing in death.

10.

O, THOU, to whose all-searching sight
  The darkness shineth as the light,
Search, prove my heart, it pants for thee;
Oh, burst these bonds, and set it free!

Wash out its stains, refine its dross,
Nail my affections to the cross;
Hallow each thought, let all within
Be clean, as thou, my Lord, art clean.

1.

VAIN man, thy fond pursuits forbear—
  Repent—thy end is nigh!
Death, at the furthest, can't be far,
  Oh, think—before thou die!

Reflect—thou hast a soul to save,
  Thy sins—how high they mount!
What are thy hopes beyond the grave—
  How stands that dread account?

To-day the Gospel calls, to-day,
  Sinner, it speaks to you;
Let every one forsake his way,
  And mercy will ensue.

2.

RETURN, O wanderer, return,
  And seek thy Father's face;
Those new desires which in thee burn,
  Were kindled by his grace.

Return, O wanderer, return;
  Thy Saviour bids thee live:
Come to his cross, and, grateful, learn
  How freely he'll forgive.

Return, O wanderer, return;
  Regain thy long-sought rest:
The Saviour's melting mercies yearn
  To clasp thee to his breast.

3.

FOREVER here my rest shall be,
  Close to thy bleeding side:
This all my hope, and all my plea,
  For me the Saviour died!

My dying Saviour, and my God,
  Fountain for guilt and sin,
Sprinkle me ever with thy blood,
  And cleanse, and keep me clean.

Wash me, and make me thus thine own;
  Wash me, and mine thou art
Wash me, but not my feet alone,
  My hands, my head, my heart.

The atonement of thy blood apply,
  Till faith to sight improve;
Till hope in full fruition die,
  And all my soul be love.

4.

WHEN I can read my title clear
  To mansions in the skies,
I'll bid farewell to every fear,
  And wipe my weeping eyes.

Cho.—We will stand the storm,
  We will anchor by and by.

Let cares like a wild deluge come,
  And storms of sorrow fall,
May I but safely reach my home,
  My God, my heaven, my all!

There shall I bathe my weary soul
  In seas of heavenly rest,
And not a wave of trouble roll
  Across my peaceful breast.

5.

WHEN all thy mercies, O my God,
  My rising soul surveys,
Transported with the view, I'm lost
  In wonder, love, and praise.

O how can words with equal warmth
  The gratitude declare,
That glows within my ravished heart?
  But thou canst read it there.

Through all eternity to thee
  A grateful song I'll raise;
But O, eternity's too short
  To utter all thy praise.

6.

AM I a soldier of the cross,—
  A foll'wer of the Lamb,—
And shall I fear to own his cause,
  Or blush to speak his name?

Are there no foes for me to face?
  Must I not stem the flood?
Is this vile world a friend to grace,
  To help me on to God?

Sure I must fight if I would reign;
  Increase my courage, Lord!
I'll bear the toil, endure the pain,
  Supported by thy word.

7.

ALAS! and did my Saviour bleed?
  And did my Sovereign die?
Would he devote that sacred head
  For such a worm as I?

Was it for crimes that I have done,
  He groaned upon the tree?
Amazing pity! grace unknown?
  And love beyond degree!

But drops of grief can ne'er repay
  The debt of love I owe;
Here, Lord, I give myself away,
  'Tis all that I can do.

8.

DEAR Father, to thy mercy-seat
  My soul for shelter flies:
'Tis here I find a safe retreat
  When storms and tempests rise.

My cheerful hope can never die,
  If thou, my God, art near;
Thy grace can raise my comforts high,
  And banish every fear.

Oh, never let my soul remove
  From this divine retreat!
Still let me trust thy power and love,
  And dwell beneath thy feet.

9.

ALL hail the power of Jesus' name,
  Let angels prostrate fall;
Bring forth the royal diadem,
  And crown him—Lord of all.

Let high-born seraphs tune the lyre,
  And as they tune it, fall
Before his face, who tunes their choir,
  And crown him—Lord of all.

Ye seed of Israel's chosen race,
  Ye ransomed of the fall:
Hail him who saves you by his grace,
  And crown him—Lord of all.

Sinners! whose love can ne'er forget,
  The wormwood and the gall,
Go, spread your trophies at his feet,
  And crown him—Lord of all.

1.

OH, for a closer walk with God,
 A calm and heavenly frame;
A light to shine upon the road
 That leads me to the Lamb.

Where is the blessedness I knew,
 When first I saw the Lord?
Where is the soul-refreshing view
 Of Jesus and his word?

Return, O, holy Dove, return,
 Sweet messenger of rest
I hate the sins that made thee mourn,
 And drove thee from my breast.

The dearest idol I have known,
 Whate'er that idol be,
Help me to tear it from thy throne,
 And worship only thee.

2.

COME, Holy Spirit, heavenly Dove,
 With all thy quick'ning powers;
Kindle a flame of sacred love
 In those cold hearts of ours.

Dear Lord! and shall we ever live
 At this poor dying rate;
Our love so faint, so cold to thee,
 And thine to us so great?

Come, Holy Spirit, heavenly Dove,
 With all thy quick'ning powers;
Come shed abroad a Saviour's love,
 And that shall kindle ours.

3.

OH, for a faith that will not shrink,
 Though pressed by every foe,
That will not tremble on the brink
 Of any earthly woe;

That will not murmur or complain
 Beneath the chast'ning rod,
But in the hour of grief or pain
 Will lean upon its God;—

Lord, give us such a faith as this,
 And then, whate'er may come,
We'll taste e'en here, the hallowed bliss
 Of an eternal home.

4.

O, FOR a heart to praise my God,
 A heart from sin set free;—
A heart that always feels thy blood,
 So freely spilt for me!

A heart resign'd, submissive, meek,
 My great Redeemer's throne;
Where only Christ is heard to speak,—
 Where Jesus reigns alone.

A heart in every thought renew'd,
 And full of love Divine;
Perfect, and right, and pure, and good,
 A copy, Lord, of thine.

Thy nature, gracious Lord, impart;
 Come quickly from above;
Write thy new name upon my heart—
 Thy new, best name of Love.

5.

FATHER, I stretch my hands to thee,
 No other help I know;
If thou withdraw thyself from me,
 Ah, whither shall I go?

Cho.—Help me, dear Saviour, thee to own,
 And ever faithful be;
And when thou sittest on thy throne,
 O Lord, remember me.

What did thine only Son endure,
 Before I drew my breath!
What pain, what labor, to secure
 My soul from endless death!

Author of faith, to thee I lift
 My weary, longing eyes;
Oh, let me now receive that gift,
 My soul without it dies.

6.

JESUS, thine all-victorious love
 Shed in my heart abroad,
Then shall my feet no longer rove,
 Rooted and fix'd in God.

O, that in me the sacred fire
 Might now begin to glow;
Burn up the dross of base desire,
 And make the mountains flow.

O, that it now from heaven might fall,
 And all my sins consume:
Come, Holy Ghost, for thee I call;
 Spirit of burning, come.

Refining fire, go through my heart;
 Illuminate my soul;
Scatter thy life through every part,
 And sanctify the whole.

7.

OH, for a thousand tongues to sing
 My great Redeemer's praise!
The glories of my God and King,
 The triumphs of his grace!

My gracious Master, and my God,
 Assist me to proclaim,
To spread through all the earth abroad,
 The honors of thy name.

He breaks the power of canceled sin,
 He sets the pris'ner free;
His blood can make the foulest clean,
 His blood availed for me.

8.

THERE is a land of pure delight,
 Where saints immortal reign;
Infinite day excludes the night,
 And pleasures banish pain.

There everlasting spring abides,
 And never with'ring flowers:
Death, like a narrow sea, divides
 This heavenly land from ours.

Sweet fields, beyond the swelling flood,
 Stand dressed in living green;
So to the Jews old Canaan stood,
 While Jordan rolled between.

Oh, could we make our doubts remove,
 The gloomy doubts that rise,
And see the Canaan that we love,
 With unbeclouded eyes.

9.

TO Father, Son and Holy Ghost,
 One God whom we adore,
Be glory as it was, is now,
 And shall be evermore.

1

RETURN and come to God;
　Cast all your sins away;
Seek ye the Saviour's cleansing blood;
　Repent, believe, obey.

Say not ye cannot come;
　For Jesus bled and died,
That none who ask in humble faith,
　Should ever be denied.

Say not ye will not come;
　'Tis God vouchsafes to call;
And fearful will their end be found,
　On whom his wrath shall fall.

Come then, whoever will,
　Come while 'tis called to-day;
Flee to the Saviour's cleansing blood,
　Repent, believe, obey.

2.

OUR sins on Christ were laid;
　He bore the mighty load;
Our ransom-price be fully paid
　In groans, and tears, and blood.

To save a world, he dies;
　Sinners, behold the Lamb!
To him lift up your longing eyes;
　Seek mercy in his name.

Jesus, we look to thee;—
　Where else can sinners go?
Thy boundless love shall set us free
　From wretchedness and woe.

3.

AND can I yet delay
　My little all to give?
To tear my soul from earth away
　For Jesus to receive?

Nay, but I yield, I yield;
　I can hold out no more:
I sink, by dying love compell'd,
　And own thee conqueror.

Though late, I all forsake;
　My friends, my all, resign:
Gracious Redeemer, take, O take,
　And seal me ever thine.

Come, and possess me whole,
　Nor hence again remove;
Settle and fix my wav'ring soul
　With all thy weight of love.

4.

DID Christ o'er sinners weep,
　And shall our cheeks be dry?
Let floods of penitential grief
　Burst forth from every eye.

The Son of God in tears,
　The wondering angels see!
Be thou astonished, O my soul!
　He shed those tears for thee.

He wept that we might weep—
　Each sin demands a tear;
In heaven alone no sin is found,
　And there's no weeping there.

5.

BEHOLD the throne of grace;
　The promise calls us near;
There Jesus shows a smiling face,
　And waits to answer prayer.

Thine image, Lord, bestow,—
　Thy presence and thy love,—
That we may serve thee here below,
　And reign with thee above.

Teach us to live by faith,
　Conform our wills to thine;
Let us victorious be in death,
　And then in glory shine.

6.

A CHARGE to keep I have,
　A God to glorify,
A never-dying soul to save
　And fit it for the sky.

To serve the present age,
　My calling to fulfill,
Oh, may it all my powers engage
　To do my Master's will.

Arm me with jealous care
　As in thy sight to live,
And, oh, thy servant, Lord, prepare
　A strict account to give.

Help me to watch and pray
　And on thyself rely,
Assured, if I my trust betray,
　I shall forever die.

7.

OH that I could repent,
　With all my idols part;
And to thy gracious eye present
　A humble contrite heart!

Jesus, on me bestow
　The penitent desire;
With true sincerity of woe
　My aching breast inspire.

With softening pity look,
　And melt my hardness down;
Strike, with thy love's resistless stroke,
　And break this heart of stone!

8.

O COME, and dwell in me,
　Spirit of power within;
And bring the glorious liberty
　From sorrow, fear, and sin!

The whole of sin's disease,
　Spirit of health, remove,—
Spirit of perfect holiness,
　Spirit of perfect love.

I want the witness, Lord,
　That all I do is right,—
According to thy will and word,—
　Well-pleasing in thy sight.

I ask no higher state;
　Indulge me but in this,
And soon or later them translate
　To my eternal bliss.

9.

COME, ye that love the Lord,
　And let your joys be known;
Join in a song with sweet accord,
　While ye surround his throne.

Let those refuse to sing,
　Who never knew our God;
But servants of the heavenly king
　May speak their joys abroad.

Then let our songs abound,
　And every tear be dry:
We're marching through Immanuel's ground,
　To fairer worlds on high.

1.

DEPTH of mercy! can there be
  Mercy still reserved for me?
Can my God his wrath forbear?
Me, the chief of sinners, spare?

I have long withstood his grace,
Long provoked him to his face;
Would not hearken to his calls:
Grieved him by a thousand falls.

Now incline me to repent!
Let me now my fall lament!
Now my foul revolt deplore!
Weep, believe, and sin no more.

2.

WHEN this song of praise shall cease,
  Let thy children, Lord, depart
With the blessing of thy peace,
And thy love in every heart.

Oh, where'er our path may lie,
Father, let us not forget
That we walk beneath thine eye,
That thy care upholds us yet.

Blind are we, and weak and frail;
Be thine aid forever near;
May the fear to sin prevail
Over every other fear.

3.

WE are waiting, blessed Lord,
  In thy courts with one accord;
At thine altars bending low,
Kindred souls together flow;
Yearning love and strong desire
To thy throne of grace aspire,
And with kindling faith we pray—
Holy Spirit, come to-day.

In the closet all alone,
Help us, Christ, to touch the throne!
As we walk, and talk, and sigh,
Hear, oh, hear thy people's cry;
Bring us nearer to thy heart—
We would dwell no more apart;
Sweep the barriers all away—
Holy Spirit, come to-day.

Come to-day—yes, come to-day!
While we wait, and weep, and pray;
Holding fast in Jesus' name
All the promise we may claim,
Come in one grand, glorious hour,
With the burning fire and power
And the wonders, long foretold,
Of the Pentecost of old!

4.

LORD, we come before thee now,
  At thy feet we humbly bow;
Oh! do not our suit disdain;
Shall we seek thee, Lord, in vain?
Lord, on thee our souls depend;
In compassion now descend;
Fill our hearts with thy rich grace,
Tune our lips to sing thy praise.

Send some message to us Lord,
That may joy and peace afford;
Let thy Spirit now impart
Full salvation to each heart.

5.

JESUS! lover of my soul,
  Let me to thy bosom fly,
While the nearer waters roll,
  While the tempest still is high;
Hide me, O my Saviour, hide,
  Till the storm of life be past;
Safe into the haven guide—
  O receive my soul at last!

Other refuge have I none;
  Hangs my helpless soul on thee;
Leave, ah! leave me not alone;
  Still support and comfort me.
All my trust on thee is stayed;
  All my help from thee I bring;
Cover my defenceless head
  With the shadow of thy wing.

Plenteous grace with thee is found—
  Grace to cover all my sin;
Let the healing streams abound,
  Make and keep me pure within.
Thou of life the fountain art;
  Freely let me take of thee:
Spring thou up within my heart,
  Rise to all eternity.

6.

CHILDREN of the heavenly King,
  As we journey let us sing;
Sing our Saviour's worthy praise,
Glorious in his works and ways.

We are trav'ling home to God,
In the way our fathers trod;
They are happy now, and we
Soon their happiness shall see.

Fear not, brethren, joyful stand
On the borders of our land;
Jesus Christ, our Father's Son,
Bids us undismayed go on.

Lord! obediently we'll go,
Gladly leaving all below;
Only thou our leader be,
And we still will follow thee!

7.

HASTE, O sinner, to be wise!
  Stay not for the morrow's sun;
Wisdom warns thee, from the skies,
  All the paths of death to shun.

Haste, and mercy now implore;
  Stay not for the morrow's sun;
Thy probation may be o'er
  Ere this evening's work is done.

Haste, while yet thou canst be blest;
  Stay not for the morrow's sun,
Death may thy poor soul arrest,
  Ere the morrow is begun.

8.

COME, my soul, thy suit prepare,
  Jesus loves to answer prayer;
He himself invites thee near,
Bids thee ask him, waits to hear.
Lord, I come to thee for rest;
Take possession of my breast;
There thy blood-bought right maintain,
And without a rival reign.

While I am a pilgrim here
Let thy love my spirit cheer;
As my guide, my guard, my friend,
Lead me to my journey's end.
Show me what I have to do;
Every hour my strength renew;
Let me live a life of faith,
Let me die thy people's death.

1

SWEET the moments, rich in blessing,
 Which before the cross I spend;
Life and health and peace possessing,
 From the sinner's dying Friend.
Here I sit, in wonder viewing
 Mercy's streams in streams of blood;
Precious drops my soul bedewing,
 Plead and claim my peace with God.

Here it is I find my heaven,
 While upon the Lamb I gaze;
Love I much? I've much forgiven;
 I'm a miracle of grace.
May I still enjoy this feeling,
 In all need to Jesus go;
Prove his death each day more healing,
 And himself more fully know.

2.

O PARADISE! O Paradise!
 Who doth not crave for rest?
Who would not seek the happy land
 Where they that loved are blest?

Ref.—I long to be where Jesus is,
 To be at home in Paradise.

O Paradise! O Paradise!
 I want to sin no more,
I want to be as pure on earth
 As on thy spotless shore.

O Paradise! O Paradise!
 I greatly long to see
The special place my dearest Lord
 In love prepares for me.

3.

ARISE, my soul, arise;
 Shake off thy guilty fears;
The bleeding Sacrifice
 In my behalf appears;
Before the throne my Surety stands,
My name is written on his hands.

The Father hears him pray,
 His dear anointed one:
He cannot turn away
 The presence of his son:
His spirit answers to the blood,
And tells me I am born of God.

My God is reconciled,
 His pard'ning voice I hear:
He owns me for his child,
 I can no longer fear;
With confidence I now draw nigh,
And Father, Abba, Father, cry.

4.

SWEET rivers of redeeming love,
 Lie just below mine eye;
Had I the pinions of a dove,
 I'd to those regions fly;
I'd rise superior to my pain,
 With joy outstrip the wind;
I'd cross bold Jordan's stormy main,
 And leave the world behind.

Oh come, my Saviour, come away,
 And bear me through the sky,
Nor let thy chariot wheels delay,
 Make haste and bring it nigh:
I long to see thy glorious face,
 And in thine image shine;
To triumph in victorious grace,
 And be forever thine.

Then I will tune my harp of gold,
 To my eternal King;
Through ages that can ne'er be told,
 I'll make his praises ring:
All hail! thou great eternal God!
 Who died on Calvary;
And saved me with his precious blood,
 From endless misery.

5.

THOU Shepherd of Israel and mine,
 The joy and desire of my heart,
For closer communion I pine,
 I long to reside where thou art;
Ah! show me that happiest place,
 The place of thy people's abode;
Where saints in an ecstacy gaze,
 And hang on a crucified Lord.

'T is there with the lambs of thy flock,
 There only I covet to rest;
To lie at the foot of the rock,
 Or rise to be hid in thy breast:
'T is there I would always abide,
 And never a moment depart:
Concealed in the cleft of thy side,
 Eternally held in thy heart.

6.

LOVE divine, all love excelling,
 Joy of heaven, to earth come down;
Fix in us thy humble dwelling,
 All thy faithful mercies crown:
Jesus, thou art all compassion;
 Pure, unbounded love thou art;
Visit us with thy salvation,
 Enter every trembling heart.

Breathe, oh breathe thy loving Spirit
 Into every troubled breast;
Let us all in thee inherit,
 Let us find that second rest;
Come, almighty to deliver,
 Let us all thy life receive;
Suddenly return, and never,
 Never more thy temples leave.

7.

COME, my fond fluttering heart,
 Come, struggle to be free,
Thou and the world must part,
 However hard it be:
My trembling spirit owns it just,
But cleaves yet closer to the dust.

Ye tempting sweets forbear,
 Ye dearest idols fall:
My love ye must not share,
 Jesus shall have it all:
'Tis bitter pain, 'tis cruel smart,
But ah! thou must consent, my heart!

But oh, there is a balm,
 A kind Physician there,
My fevered mind to calm,
 To bid me not despair:
Aid me, dear Saviour, set me free,
And I will all resign to thee.

8.

MAY the grace of Christ our Saviour,
 And the Father's boundless love,
With the Holy Spirit's favor,
 Rest upon us from above.
Thus may we abide in union
 With each other and the Lord,
And possess, in sweet communion,
 Joys which earth cannot afford.

1.

MY faith looks up to thee,
Thou Lamb of Calvary;
Saviour divine;
Now hear me while I pray;
Take all my guilt away;
Oh let me, from this day,
Be wholly thine.

May thy rich grace impart,
Strength to my fainting heart;
My zeal inspire;
As thou hast died for me,
Oh may my love to thee,
Pure, warm and changeless be—
A living fire.

While life's dark maze I tread,
And grief around me spread,
Be thou my guide;
Bid darkness turn to day;
Wipe sorrow's tears away,
Nor let me ever stray
From thee aside.

2.

NEARER, my God, to thee,
Nearer to thee:
E'en though it be a cross
That raiseth me;
Still all my song shall be,
Nearer, my God, to thee,
Nearer to thee.

Though like a wanderer,
Daylight all gone,
Darkness be over me,
My rest a stone,
Yet in my dreams I'd be
Nearer, my God, to thee, etc.

There let the way appear
Steps up to heaven;
All that thou sendest me,
In mercy given,
Angels to beckon me
Nearer, my God, to thee, etc.

3.

ROCK of Ages, cleft for me,
Let me hide myself in thee;
Let the water and the blood,
From thy wounded side which flow'd,
Be of sin the double cure,—
Save from wrath and make me pure.

Could my tears forever flow,
Could my zeal no languor know,
These for sin could not atone;
Thou must save, and thou alone:
In my hand no price I bring;
Simply to the cross I cling.

While I draw this fleeting breath,
When my eyes shall close in death,
When I rise to worlds unknown,
And behold thee on thy throne,
Rock of Ages, cleft for me,
Let me hide myself in thee.

4.

BLESSED Jesus, thou art mine,
All I have is wholly thine;
Thou dost dwell within my heart,
Thou dost reign in every part;
Blessed Jesus, keep me white,
Keep me walking in the light.

I am safe within the fold,
All my cares on thee are rolled,
I enjoy the sweetest rest,
For I'm leaning on thy breast;
Blessed Jesus, keep me white,
Keep me walking in the light.

Precious Jesus, day by day,
Keep me in the holy way;
Keep my mind in perfect peace;
Every day my faith increase:
Blessed Jesus, keep me white,
Keep me walking in the light.

5.

TAKE my life and let it be
Consecrated, Lord to thee.
Take my hands and let them move
At the impulse of thy love.

REFRAIN.

Take myself and let me be
Ever only all for thee.

Take my moments and my days,
Let them flow in ceaseless praise.
Take my will and make it thine,
Let it be no longer mine.

Take my heart, it is thine own,
Let it be thy royal throne.
Take my love, my Lord of power,
At thy feet its treasures store.

6.

WHEN shall we meet again,
Meet ne'er to sever?
When will peace wreathe her chain
Round us forever?
Our hearts will ne'er repose,
Safe from each blast that blows,
In this dark vale of woes,
Never—no, never!

When shall love freely flow
Pure as life's river?
When shall sweet friendship glow
Changeless forever?
Where joys celestial thrill,
Where bliss each heart shall fill,
And fears of parting chill
Never—no, never!

Up to that world of light
Take us, dear Saviour;
May we all there unite,
Happy forever;
Where kindred spirits dwell,
There may our music swell,
And time our joys dispel
Never—no, never!

7.

COME, Holy Ghost, in love,
Shed on us from above
Thine own bright ray!
Divinely good thou art;
Thy sacred gifts impart
To gladden each sad heart:
O come to-day!

Come, tenderest Friend, and best,
Our most delightful Guest,
With soothing power:
Rest, which the weary know,
Shade, 'mid the noontide glow,
Peace, when deep griefs o'erflow,
Cheer us this hour!

Come, Light serene, and still,
Our inmost bosoms fill;
Dwell in each breast;
We know no dawn but thine,
Send forth thy beams divine,
On our dark souls to shine,
And make us blest!

1.

COME, ye sinners, poor and needy,
  Weak and wounded, sick and sore,
Jesus ready stands to save you,
  Full of pity, love and power:
    He is able,
He is willing, doubt no more.

Now ye needy, come and welcome,
  God's free bounty glorify;
True belief and true repentance,
  Every grace that brings you nigh,
    Without money,
Come to Jesus Christ and buy.

Come, ye weary, heavy-laden,
  Bruised and mangled by the fall,
If you tarry till you're better,
  You will never come at all;
    Not the righteous,
Sinners, Jesus came to call.

2.

OH, thou God of my salvation,
  My Redeemer from all sin;
Moved by thy divine compassion,
  Who hast died my heart to win;
Where shall I thy praise begin?

Though unseen, I love the Saviour;
  He hath brought salvation near;
Manifests his pard'ning favor;
  And when Jesus doth appear,
  Soul and body
Shall his glorious image bear.

Angels now are hov'ring round us,
  Unperceived amid the throng;
Wond'ring at the love that crowned us,
  Glad to join the holy song;
    Hallelujah,
Love and praise to Christ belong!

3.

COME thou fount of every blessing,
  Tune my heart to sing thy grace;
Streams of mercy, never ceasing,
  Call for songs of loudest praise,
Teach me some melodious sonnet,
  Sung by flaming tongues above;
Praise the mount—I'm fixed upon it,
  Mount of thy redeeming love.

Here I'll raise mine Ebenezer;
  Hither by thy help I'm come;
And I hope by thy good pleasure,
  Safely to arrive at home.
Jesus sought me when a stranger,
  Wand'ring from the fold of God;
He, to rescue me from danger,
  Interposed his precious blood.

Oh, to grace how great a debtor
  Daily I'm constrained to be!
Let thy goodness like a fetter,
  Bind my wand'ring heart to thee.
Prone to wander, Lord, I feel it—
  Prone to leave the God I love;
Here's my heart, oh take and seal it—
  Seal it for thy courts above.

4.

LORD, dismiss us with thy blessing;
  Fill our hearts with joy and peace;
Let us each, thy love possessing,
  Triumph in redeeming grace;
    Oh refresh us,
Traveling through this wilderness.

Thanks we give, and adoration,
  For thy gospel's joyful sound;
May the fruits of thy salvation
  In our hearts and lives abound;
    May thy presence
With us evermore be found.

So, when'er the signal's given,
  Us from earth to call away,
Borne on angels' wings to heaven,
  Glad the summons to obey,
    May we ever
Reign with Christ in endless day.

5.

NOW the solemn shadows darken,
  And the daylight slowly dies,
Holy Saviour, thou wilt hearken
  When thy children's prayers arise,
    Blessed Jesus!
Look on us with loving eyes.

Some are tried with doubts and dangers,
  Some have found their hearts grow cold
Some are aliens now, and strangers
  To the faith they loved of old;
    Blessed Jesus!
Bring them back into thy fold.

Some in conflict sore have striven
  With temptation fierce and strong;
Lord, to them let strength be given
  If the battle should be long!
    Blessed Jesus!
Change our mourning into song.

6.

IN the cross of Christ I glory,
  Towering o'er the wrecks of time;
All the light of sacred story
  Gathers round its head sublime.

When the woes of life o'ertake me,
  Hopes deceive, and fears annoy,
Never shall the cross forsake me;
  Lo! it glows with peace and joy.

Bane and blessing, pain and pleasure,
  By the cross are sanctified;
Peace is there, that knows no measure,
  Joys, that through all time abide.

7.

STAND up!—stand up for Jesus!
  Ye soldiers of the cross;
Lift high his royal banner,
  It must not suffer loss;
From victory unto victory
  His army shall be led,
Till every foe is vanquished,
  And Christ is Lord indeed.

Stand up!—stand up for Jesus!
  Stand in his strength alone;
The arm of flesh will fail you—
  Ye dare not trust your own;
Put on the gospel armor,
  And, watching unto prayer,
Where duty calls or danger,
  Be never wanting there.

Stand up!—stand up for Jesus!
  The strife will not be long;
This day the noise of battle,
  The next the victor's song;
To him that overcometh,
  A crown of life shall be;
He, with the King of glory,
  Shall reign eternally.

1.

I HAVE entered the valley of blessing
so sweet,
And Jesus abides with me there;
And his Spirit and blood make my cleans-
ing complete,
And his perfect love casteth out fear.

Cho.—O come to this valley of blessing so sweet,
Where Jesus will fullness bestow,
And believe, and receive, and confess him,
That all his salvation may know.

There is love in the valley of blessing so
sweet,
Such as none but the blood-washed may
feel;
When heaven comes down redeemed spirits
to greet,
And Christ sets his covenant seal.

There's a song in the valley of blessing so
sweet,
That angels would fain join the strain;
As with rapturous praises we bow at his feet,
Crying, Worthy the Lamb that was slain.

2.

I HAVE a Saviour, he's pleading in glory,
A dear, loving Saviour though earth-
friends be few;
And now he is watching in tenderness o'er
me,
And oh that my Saviour were your
Saviour too!

Cho.—For you I am praying,
For you I am praying,
For you I am praying,
I'm praying for you.

I have a Father: to me he has given
A hope for eternity, blessed and true;
And soon will he call me to meet him in
heaven,
But oh that he'd let me bring you with
me too!

I have a peace: it is calm as a river—
A peace that the friends of this world
never knew;
My Saviour alone is its Author and Giver,
And oh, could I know it was given to you!

3.

THERE'S a wideness in God's mercy,
Like the wideness of the sea;
There's a kindness in his justice,
Which is more than liberty.

Cho.—He is calling, "Come to me;"
Lord, I'll gladly haste to thee.

There is welcome for the sinner
And more graces for the good;
There is mercy for the Saviour;
There is healing in his blood.

If our love were but more simple,
We should take him at his word;
And our lives would be all sunshine
In the sweetness of our Lord.

4.

O BLISS of the purified! bliss of the free!
I plunge in the crimson tide open'd
for me!
O'er sin and uncleanness exulting I stand,
And point to the print of the nails in his
hand.

Cho.—O! sing of his mighty love—mighty
to save.

O bliss of the purified, Jesus is mine,
No longer in dread condemnation I pine:
In conscious salvation I sing of his grace
Who lifted upon me the smiles of his face!

O bliss of the purified! bliss of the pure;
No wound hath the soul that his blood
cannot cure;
No sorrow-bowed head but may sweetly
find rest,
No tears—but may dry them on Jesus's
breast.

5.

I KNOW not if the dark or bright
Shall be my lot,
If that wherein my soul delight
Be best or not;
It may be mine to drag for years
Toil's heavy chain,
Or day and night my meat be tears,
On bed of pain.

Chorus.

But this I know, there is a hand divine
That holds me still, whatever lot be mine;
But this I know, where'er I go, there is a
hand divine,
That holds me still, thro' every ill, what-
ever lot be mine.

My bark is wafted to the strand
By breath divine,
And on the helm there rests a hand
More strong than mine;
One who has known in storms to sail
I have on board;
Above the raging of the gale,
I hear my Lord.

He holds me 'midst the billows' might,
I shall not fall;
If sharp, 'tis short; if long, 'tis light;
He tempers all—
Safe to the land, safe to the land,
The end is this:
And then with him go hand in hand,
Far into bliss.

6.

SAVIOUR, like a shepherd lead us;
Much we need thy tend'rest care;
In thy pleasant pastures feed us,
For our use thy folds prepare.
Blessed Jesus, thou hast bought us, thine we are.

We are thine, do thou befriend us;
Be the guardian of our way;
Keep thy flock, from sin defend us,
Seek us when we go astray.
Blessed Jesus, hear, O hear us when we pray.

Thou hast promised to receive us,
Poor and sinful though we be;
Thou hast mercy to relieve us,
Grace to cleanse, and power to free.
Blessed Jesus, we will early turn to thee.

7.

PRAISE the name of God most high,
Praise him, all below the sky,
Praise him, all ye heavenly host,
Father, Son and Holy Ghost;
As through countless ages past,
Evermore his praise shall last.

1.

IN some way or other the Lord will provide:
   It may not be *my* way,
   It may not be *thy* way;
   And yet, in his *own* way,
   "The Lord will provide."

Cho.—Then we'll trust in the Lord,
   And he will provide;
   Yes, we'll trust in the Lord,
   And he will provide.

At some time or other the Lord will provide:
   It may not be *my* time,
   It may not be *thy* time;
   And yet in his *own* time,
   "The Lord will provide."

Despond then no longer: the Lord will provide;
   And this be the token—
   No word he hath spoken
   Was ever yet broken:
   "The Lord will provide."

2.

PRECIOUS promise God hath given
   To the weary passer by,
On the way from earth to heaven,
   "I will guide thee with mine eye."

Cho.—I will guide thee, I will guide thee,
   I will guide thee with mine eye;
   On the way from earth to heaven,
   I will guide thee with mine eye.

When temptations almost win thee,
   And thy trusted watchers fly,
Let this promise ring within thee,
   "I will guide thee with mine eye."

When thy secret hopes have perished,
   In the grave of years gone by,
Let this promise still be cherished,
   "I will guide thee with mine eye."

3.

WE speak of the realms of the blessed,
   That country so bright and so fair;
And oft are its glories confessed,
   But what must it be to be there.

Cho.—Over there, over there,
   O, what must it be to be there.

We speak of its freedom from sin,
   From sorrow, temptation and care,
From trials without and within—
   But what must it be to be there!

Do thou, Lord, mid'st pleasure or woe
   For heaven my spirit prepare;
And shortly I also shall know,
   And feel what it is to be there.

4.

I LEFT it all with Jesus Long ago;
   All my sins I brought him, And my woe,
When by faith I saw him On the tree,
Heard his small, still whisper, "'Tis for thee;
From my heart the burden Rolled away—
   Happy day.

I leave it all with Jesus Day by day;
Faith can firmly trust him Come what may.
Hope has dropped her anchor, Found her rest
In the calm, sure haven Of his breast;
Love esteems it heaven To abide
   At his side.

O, leave it all with Jesus, Drooping soul!
Tell not half the story, But the whole;
Worlds on worlds are hanging On his hand,
Life and death are waiting His command;
Yet his tender bosom Makes thee room—
   O come home!

5.

I LOVE to tell the story
   Of unseen things above,
Of Jesus and his glory,
   Of Jesus and his love;
I love to tell the story,
   Because I know it's true,
It satisfies my longings,
   As nothing else would do.

Cho.—I love to tell the story,
   'Twill be my theme in glory
   To tell the old, old story,
   Of Jesus and his love.

I love to tell the story;
   More wonderful it seems
Than all the golden fancies
   Of all our golden dreams,
I love to tell the story;
   It did so much for me!
And that is just the reason
   I tell it now to thee.

6.

I LAY my sins on Jesus, The spotless Lamb of God;
He bears them all and frees us From the accursed load.

Cho.—Hallelujah, Jesus saves me, He makes me "white as snow."

I bring my guilt to Jesus, To wash my crimson stains
White, in his blood most precious, Till not a spot remains.

I lay my wants on Jesus—All fullness dwells in him;
He healeth my diseases, He doth my soul redeem.

7.

THERE'S a highway for the ransomed,
   where the children of the King,
Upon their pilgrim journey triumphantly may sing,
Of a Saviour who redeemed them, and delivers from all sin.
   His blood NOW makes me clean.

Cho.—Glory, glory, hallelujah!
   Glory, glory, hallelujah!
   Glory, glory, hallelujah!
   His blood NOW keeps me clean.

I was pardoned by God's mercy, but at heart was evil still,
A carnal mind was in me, which resolves could never kill.
But, blessed be his holy name, he changes heart and will!
   His blood NOW makes me clean.

Now, like pebbles in the running brook that 'neath the ripples lay,
My heart is sweetly kept from sin each moment, night and day;
And as faith the conquest gave me, I bid doubts to go their way,
   His blood NOW makes me clean!

On the mountain tops of Beulah or in the vale below,
Where temptations' wildest hurricanes their fiercest tempests blow,
In sorrow or in conflict his grace he doth bestow,
   His blood NOW makes me clean!

1.

TELL me the old, old story,
  Of unseen things above;
Of Jesus and his glory,
  Of Jesus and his love.
Tell me the story simply,
  As to a little child;
For I am weak and weary,
  And helpless and defiled.

Cho.—Tell me the old, old story,
  Of Jesus and his love.

Tell me the story slowly,
  That I may take it in;
That wonderful redemption,
  God's remedy for sin.
Tell me the story often,
  For I forget so soon,
The "early dew" of morning
  Has passed away at noon.

Tell me the story softly,
  With earnest tones, and grave;
Remember, I'm the sinner
  Whom Jesus came to save;
Tell me the story always,
  If you would really be
In any time of trouble
  A comforter to me.

2.

IN the Christian's home in glory,
  There remains a land of rest.
Where the Saviour's gone before me
  To fulfill my soul's request.

Cho.—On the other side of Jordan,
  In the sweet fields of Eden,
  Where the tree of life is blooming,
  There is rest for you.
  There is rest for the weary,
  There is rest for you.

Pain or sickness ne'er can enter;
  Grief nor woe my lot shall share;
But in that celestial center
  I, a crown of life shall wear.

Sing, O sing, ye heirs of glory,
  Shout your triumph as you go;
Zion's gates will open to you,
  You shall find an entrance through.

3.

HE leadeth me! oh! blessed thought;
  Oh! words with heav'nly comfort fraught;
Whate'er I do, where'er I be,
Still 'tis God's hand that leadeth me.

Ref.—He leadeth me, He leadeth me!
  By his own hand he leadeth me;
  His faithful follower I would be,
  For by his hand he leadeth me.

Sometimes 'mid scenes of deepest gloom,
Sometimes where Eden's bowers bloom,
By waters still, o'er troubled sea,—
Still 'tis his hand that leadeth me.

Lord, I would clasp thy hand in mine,
Nor ever murmur nor repine—
Content, whatever lot I see,
Since 'tis my God that leadeth me.

4.

ALL glory to the bleeding lamb,
  Who died on Calvary!
Yes, glory to the bleeding Lamb
Who saves and ransoms me!

Cho.—I've been redeem'd, I've been redeem'd,
  Been wash'd in the blood of the Lamb,
  Been redeem'd by the blood of the Lamb,
  That flow'd on Calvary.

The blood that my Redeemer spilt,
  The blood, so rich and free,
That cleanses sinful heart from guilt,
  Now saves and cleanses me.

I am redeemed—O blessed state!
  I am redeemed from sin,
O, love so infinitely great!
  The blood has made me clean.

5.

THERE were ninety and nine that safely lay
  In the shelter of the fold,
But one was out on the hills away,
  Far off from the gates of gold—
Away on the mountains wild and bare,
Away from the tender Shepherd's care.

"Lord, thou hast here thy ninety and nine;
  Are they not enough for thee?"
But the Shepherd made answer: "This of mine
  Has wandered away from me:
And although the road be rough and steep,
I go to the desert to find my sheep."

But none of the ransomed ever knew
  How deep were the waters crossed;
Nor how dark was the night that the Lord passed through
Ere he found his sheep that was lost.
Out in the desert he heard its cry—
Sick and helpless, and ready to die.

But all through the mountains, thunder-riven,
  And up from the rocky steep,
There rose a cry to the gate of heaven,
  "Rejoice! I have found my sheep!"
And the angels echoed around the throne,
  "Rejoice, for the Lord brings back his own!"

6.

SOWING the seed by the day-light fair,
  Sowing the seed by the noon-day glare,
Sowing the seed by the fading light,
Sowing the seed in the solemn night,
:|: Oh, what shall the harvest be? :|:

Cho.—Sown in the darkness or sown in the light,
  Sown in our weakness or sown in our might,
  Gathered in time or eternity,
  Sure, ah, sure will the harvest, harvest be.

Sowing the seed by the way-side high,
Sowing the seed on the rock to die,
Sowing the seed where the thorns will spoil,
Sowing the seed in the fertile soil,
:|: Oh, what shall the harvest be? :|:

Sowing the seed with an aching heart,
Sowing the seed while the teardrops start,
Sowing in hope till the reapers come
Gladly to gather the harvest home,
:|: Oh, what shall the harvest be? :|:

1.

I GAVE my life for thee
  My precious blood I shed,
That thou might'st ransomed be,
  And quickened from the dead;
I gave, I gave my life for thee,
What hast thou given for me?

My Father's house of light,—
  My glory-circled throne,
I left, for earthly night,
  For wand'rings sad and lone;
I left, I left it all for thee;
Hast thou left aught for me?

And I have brought to thee,
  Down from my home above,
Salvation full and free,
  My pardon and my love;
I bring, I bring rich gifts to thee,
What hast thou brought to me.

2.

WHAT a friend we have in Jesus,
  All our sins and griefs to bear;
What a privilege to carry
  Everything to God in prayer,
O, what peace we often forfeit,
  O, what needless pain we bear—
All because we do not carry
  Everything to God in prayer.

Have we trials and temptations?
  Is there trouble anywhere?
We should never be discouraged,
  Take it to the Lord in prayer.
Can we find a Friend so faithful,
  Who will all our sorrows share?
Jesus knows our every weakness,
  Take it to the Lord in prayer.

Are we weak and heavy laden,
  Cumbered with a load of care?
Precious Saviour, still our refuge,
  Take it to the Lord in prayer.
Do thy friends despise, forsake thee?
  Take it to the Lord in prayer;
In his arms he'll take and shield thee,
  Thou wilt find a solace there.

3.

LORD, I hear of showers of blessing
  Thou art scatt'ring full and free;
Showers, the thirsty land refreshing;
  Let some droppings fall on me—Even me.

Love of God—so pure and changeless;
  Blood of Christ—so rich and free;
Grace of God—so strong and boundless;
  Magnify it all in me—Even me.

Pass me not—thy lost one bringing;
  Bend my heart, O Lord, to thee;
Whilst the streams of life are springing,
  Blessing others, O, bless me—Even me.

4.

THERE is life for a look at the crucified One,
There is life at this moment for thee:
Then look, sinner, look unto him and be saved,
Unto him who was nailed to the tree.

Ref.—Look! look! look and live!
  There is life for a look at the crucified One,
  There is life at this moment for thee.

It is not thy tears of repentance and prayers,
  But the blood that atones for the soul;
On him, then, who shed it, thou mayest at once
  Thy weight of iniquities roll.

Then take with rejoicing from Jesus at once
  The life everlasting he gives;
And know with assurance thou never canst die
  Since Jesus, thy righteousness, lives.

5.

WE praise thee, O God! for the Son of thy love,
For Jesus, who died, and is now gone above.

Cho.—Hallelujah! Thine the glory, Hallelujah! amen. etc.

We praise thee, O God! for thy Spirit of light,
Who has shown us our Saviour, and scattered our night.

All glory and praise, to the Lamb that was slain,
Who has borne all our sins and has cleansed every stain.

All glory and praise to the God of all grace,
Who has bought us, and sought us, and guided our ways.

6.

COME, my Redeemer, come,
  And deign to dwell with me;
Come, and thy right assume,
  And bid thy rivals flee;
Come, my Redeemer, quickly come,
And make my heart thy lasting home.

Cho.—Whiter than snow, whiter than snow,
  Wash me in the blood of the Lamb,
  And I shall be whiter than snow.

Exert thy mighty power,
  And banish all my sin;
In this auspicious hour,
  Bring all thy graces in:
Come, my Redeemer, quickly come,
And make my heart thy lasting home.

Rule thou in every thought
  And passion of my soul,
Till all my powers are brought
  Beneath thy full control:
Come, my Redeemer, quickly come,
And make my heart thy lasting home.

7.

TO-DAY the Saviour calls;
  Ye wand'rers come!
O, ye benighted souls,
  Why longer roam?

To-day the Saviour calls!
  For refuge fly;
The storm of vengence falls,
  Ruin is nigh.

To-day the Saviour calls!
  Oh, listen now!
Within these sacred walls
  To Jesus bow.

The Spirit calls to-day;
  Yield to his power;
Oh, grieve him not away!
  'Tis mercy's hour.

1.

SWEET hour of prayer! sweet hour of prayer!
That calls me from a world of care,
And bids me at my Father's throne,
Make all my wants and wishes known.
In seasons of distress and grief,
My soul has often found relief;
And oft escaped the tempter's snare,
By thy return, sweet hour of prayer.

Sweet hour of prayer! sweet hour of prayer!
Thy wings shall my petitions bear
To him whose truth and faithfulness
Engage the waiting soul to bless:
And since he bids me seek his face,
Believe his word, and trust his grace,
I'll cast on him my every care,
And wait for thee, sweet hour of prayer.

2.

BEHOLD a stranger at the door!
He gently knocks, has knocked before,
Has waited long, is waiting still;
You treat no other friend so ill.
Cho.—Oh, let the dear Saviour come in,
He'll cleanse thy heart from sin!
Oh, keep him no more out at the door,
But let the dear Saviour come in.

Oh, lovely attitude!—he stands
With melting heart, and loaded hands,
Oh, matchless kindness!—and he shows
This matchless kindness to his foes!

But will he prove a friend indeed?
He will—the very friend you need;
The friend of sinners—yes, 'tis he,
With garments dyed on Calvary.

Rise, touched with gratitude divine,
Turn out his enemy and thine,—
That soul destroying monster, sin,—
And let the heavenly stranger in.

3.

I AM thine own, O Christ—
Henceforth entirely thine;
And life from this glad hour,
New life is mine!

Cho.—O, peace! O, holy rest,
O, balmy breath of love!
O, heart divinest, best,
Thy depth I prove.

No earthly joy shall lure
My quiet soul from thee:
This deep delight, so pure,
Is heav'n to me.

I cannot tell the art
By which such bliss is given:
I know thou hast my heart,
And I—have heaven!

4.

MY hope is built on nothing less
Than Jesus' blood and righteousness;
I dare not trust the sweetest frame,
But wholly lean on Jesus' name.

On Christ, the solid Rock, I stand,
All other ground is sinking sand.

When darkness seems to vail his face,
I rest on his unchanging grace;
In every high and stormy gale
My anchor holds within the vail.

His oath, his covenant, and blood,
Support me in the 'whelming flood:
When all around my soul gives way,
He then is all my hope and stay.

5.

O, TO be nothing, nothing,
Only to lie at his feet,
A broken and emptied vessel,
For the Master's use made meet.
Emptied that he might fill me
As forth to his service I go;
Broken, that so unhindered,
His life through me might flow.

O, to be nothing, nothing,
Only as led by his hand;
A messenger at his gateway,
Only waiting for his command;
Only an instrument ready
His praises to sound at his will,
Willing, should he not require me
In silence to wait on him still.

O, to be nothing, nothing,
Painful the humbling may be:
Yet low in the dust I'd lay me
That the world might my Saviour see.
Rather be nothing, nothing,—
To him let their voices be raised;
He is the Fountain of blessing,
He only is most to be praised.

6.

I STAND all bewildered with wonder,
And gaze on the ocean of love;
And over its waves to my spirit
Come peace, like a heavenly dove.

Cho.—The cross now covers my sins,
The past is under the blood;
I'm trusting in Jesus for all,
My will is the will of my God.

I struggled and wrestled to win it,
The blessing that setteth me free;
But, when I had ceased from my struggles,
His peace Jesus gave unto me.

He laid his hand on me and heal'd me,
And bade me be every whit whole;
I touched but the hem of his garment,
And glory came thrilling my soul.

7.

O JESUS, delight of my soul,
My Saviour, my Shepherd divine,
I yield to thy blessed control;
My body and spirit are thine:
Thy love I can never deserve,
That bids me be happy in thee;
My God and my King I will serve,
Whose favor is heaven to me.

How can I thy goodness repay,
By nature so weak and defiled?
Myself I have given away;
Oh, call me thine own blessed child;
And art thou my Father above?
Will Jesus abide in my heart?
Oh, bind me so fast with thy love,
That I from thee ne'er shall depart.

8.

TO thee be praise forever,
Thou glorious King of kings;
Thy wondrous love and favor
Each ransomed spirit sings;
We'll celebrate thy glory
With all thy saints above,
And shout the joyful story
Of thy redeeming love.

1.

YI...here is room! the Lamb's bright hall
    of song,
Wit...ts fair glory, beckons thee along;
Roo...room, still room! Oh, enter, enter
    now!
Yet...re is room! Still open stands the gate,
The...e of love; it is not yet too late;
Roo...room, still room! oh, enter, enter
    now!
Pas..., pass in! that banquet is for thee;
Th...p of everlasting love is free;
Roo...room, still room! oh, enter, enter
    now.
Ere...ght that gate may close and seal thy
    doom;
The...he last, low, long cry, "No room, no
    room!"
No r...m, no room; oh, woeful cry, "No
    room!"

2.

JESUS saves me every day,
    Jesus saves me every night;
Jesus saves me all the way,
Thro' the darkness, thro' the light.

Cho.—Jesus saves, O bliss sublime,
    Jesus saves me all the time.

Jesus saves me, he is mine;
    Jesus saves me, I am his;
Jesus saves while I recline
    On his precious promises.

Jesus saves, he saves from sin;
    Jesus saves, I feel him nigh;
Jesus saves, he dwells within;
    Gladly do I testify.

3.

PRECIOUS Saviour thou dost save me;
    Thine, and only thine I am.
Oh! the cleansing blood has reached me;
    Glory, glory to the Lamb.

Glory, glory, Jesus saves me; Glory, glory
    to the Lamb!
Oh! the cleansing blood has reached me;
    Glory, glory to the Lamb!

Long my yearning heart was trying
    To enjoy this perfect rest;
But I gave all trying over;
    Simply trusting, I was blest.

Consecrated to thy service,
    I will live and die for thee;
I will witness to thy glory,
    Of salvation full and free.

4.

YIELD not to temptation,
    For yielding is sin;
Each victory will help you
    Some other to win;
Fight manfully onward,
    Dark passions subdue,
Look ever to Jesus,
    He'll carry you through.

Cho.—Ask the Saviour to help you,
    Comfort, strengthen and keep you;
He is willing to aid you,
    He'll carry you through.

Shun evil companions,
    Bad language disdain,
God's name hold in rev'rence,
    Nor take it in vain;
Be thoughtful and earnest,
    Kind-hearted and true,
Look ever to Jesus,
    He'll carry you through.

To him that o'ercometh,
    God giveth a crown,
Thro' faith we shall conquer,
    Though often cast down;
He, who is our Saviour,
    Our strength will renew,
Look ever to Jesus,
    He'll carry you through.

5.

THERE is a spot to me more dear
    Than native vale or mountain;
A spot for which affection's tear
    Springs grateful from its fountain:
'Tis not where kindred souls abound,
    Though that is almost heaven;
But where I first my Saviour found,
    And felt my sins forgiven.

Sinking and panting as for breath,
    I knew not help was near me;
And cried "Oh! save me, Lord, from death,
    Immortal Jesus, hear me."
Then quick as thought I felt him mine,
    My Saviour stood before me;
I saw his brightness round me shine,
    And shouted, "Glory! Glory!"

O sacred hour! O hallowed spot!
    Where love divine first found me;
Wherever falls my distant lot,
    My heart shall linger round thee;
And when from earth I rise to soar
    Up to my home in heaven,
Down will I cast my eyes once more,
    Where I was first forgiven.

6.

I'M but a stranger here—
    Heaven is my home;
Earth is a desert drear—
    Heaven is my home;
Danger and sorrow stand
    Round me on every hand—
Heaven is my fatherland;
    Heaven is my home.

What though the tempests rage?
    Heaven is my home;
Short is my pilgrimage—
    Heaven is my home;
And time's wild, wintry blast
    Soon will be overpast;
I shall reach home at last—
    Heaven is my home.

7.

MY heavenly home is bright and fair;
    Nor pain, nor death can enter there;
Its glittering towers the sun outshine;
    That heavenly mansion shall me mine.

Cho.—We're going home, to die no more.

My Father's house is built on high,
    Far, far above the starry sky:
When from this earthly prison free,
    That heavenly mansion mine shall be.

Let others seek a home below
    Which flames devour, or waves o'erflow;
Be mine the happier lot to own
    A heavenly mansion near the throne.

1

JESUS, let thy pitying eye
  Call back a wand'ring sheep:
False to thee, like Peter, I
  Would fain like Peter weep.
Let me be by grace restored:
  On me be all long-suff'ring shown;
Turn, and look upon me. Lord,
  And break my heart of stone.

Saviour, Prince, enthroned above,
  Repentance to impart,
Give me through thy dying love,
  The humble, contrite heart:
Give me, what I have long implored,
  True penitence for sins unknown:
Turn, and look upon me, Lord,
  And break my heart of stone.

For thine own compassion's sake,
  The gracious wonder show;
Cast my sins behind thy back,
  And wash me white as snow;
Speak the reconciling word,
  And let thy mercy melt me down;
Turn, and look upon me, Lord,
  And break my heart of stone.

2

BY thy birth, and by thy tears;
  By thy human griefs and fears;
By thy conflict in the hour
Of the subtle tempter's power—
Saviour, look with pitying eye;
Saviour, help me, or I die.

By thy lonely hour of prayer;
By the fearful conflict there;
By thy cross and dying cries;
By thy one great sacrifice,—
Saviour, look with pitying eye;
Saviour, help me, or I die.

By thy triumph o'er the grave;
By thy power the lost to save;
By thy high, majestic throne;
By the empire all thine own,—
Saviour, look with pitying eye;
Saviour, help me, or I die.

3

HOW tedious and tasteless the hours,
  When Jesus no longer I see;
Sweet prospects, sweet birds, and sweet flowers
  Have all lost their sweetness to me:
The midsummer sun shines but dim,
  The fields strive in vain to look gay;
But when I am happy in him,
  December's as pleasant as May.

His name yields the richest perfume,
  And sweeter than music his voice;
His presence disperses my gloom,
  And makes all within me rejoice;
I should, were he always thus nigh,
  Have nothing to wish or to fear,
No mortal so happy as I,
  My summer would last all the year.

4

DEAR Jesus, I long to be perfectly whole;
  I want thee forever to live in my soul;
Break down every idol, cast out every foe;
Now wash me, and I shall be whiter than snow.

Whiter than snow, yes, whiter than snow,
Now wash me, and I shall be whiter than snow.

Dear Jesus, let nothing unholy remain;
Apply thine own blood and extract every stain;
To have this blest cleansing, I all things forego;
Now wash me and I shall be whiter than snow.

The blessing by faith I receive from above,
O, glory! my soul is made perfect in love;
My prayer has prevailed, and this moment I know
The blood is applied—I am whiter than snow.

5

MY body, soul, and spirit, Jesus, I give to thee,
  A consecrated off'ring, thine evermore to be.

Cho.—My all is on the altar, I'm waiting for the fire;
  Waiting, waiting, waiting, I'm waiting for the fire.

O! let the fire descending just now upon my soul,
Consume my humble offering, And cleanse and make me whole.

I'm thine, O blessed Jesus, Washed by thy precious blood,
Now seal me by thy Spirit, A sacrifice to God.

6

WHAT means this eager, anxious throng,
  Which moves with busy haste along—
These wondrous gatherings day by day?
What means this strange commotion, pray?
In accents hush'd the throng reply;
"Jesus of Nazareth passeth by."

Ho! all ye heavy laden come:
Here's pardon, comfort, rest, and home,
Ye wanderers from a Father's face,
Return, accept his proffered grace,
Ye tempted ones, there's refuge nigh,
"Jesus of Nazareth passeth by."

But if you still this call refuse,
And all his wondrous love abuse,
Soon will he sadly from you turn,
Your bitter prayer for pardon spurn,
"Too late! too late!" will be the cry—
"Jesus of Nazareth *has passed by.*"

7

THERE is a fountain filled with blood,
  Drawn from Immanuel's veins,
And sinners plunged beneath that flood
  Lose all their guilty stains.

The dying thief rejoiced to see
  That fountain in his day;
And there may I, though vile as he,
  Wash all my sins away.

Thou dying Lamb! thy precious blood
  Shall never lose its power,
Till all the ransomed Church of God
  Are saved to sin no more.

E'er since by faith I saw the stream
  Thy flowing wounds supply,
Redeeming love has been my theme,
  And shall be till I die.

Then in a nobler, sweeter song
  I'll sing Thy power to save,
When this poor, lisping, stammering tongue
  Lies silent in the grave.

1.

THE mistakes of my life have been many,
 The sins of my heart have been more,
And I scarce can see for weeping,
But I'll knock at the open door.

Cho.—I know I am weak and sinful,
 It comes to me more and more;
But when the dear Saviour shall bid
  me come in,
 I'll enter the open door.

I am lowest of those who love him,
 I am weakest of those who pray;
But I come as he has bidden,
 And he will not say me nay.

My mistakes his free grace will cover,
 My sins he will wash away,
And the feet that shrink and falter
 Shall walk thro' the gates of day.

The mistakes of my life have been many,
 And my spirit is sick with sin,
And I scarce can see for weeping,
 But the Saviour will let me in.

2.

JESUS, my cross have taken,
 All to leave and follow thee:
Naked, poor, despised, forsaken,
 Thou from hence my all shalt be.
Perish every fond ambition,
 All I've sought, or hoped, or known;
Yet how rich is my condition!
 God and heaven are still my own.

Let the world despise and leave me,
 They have left my Saviour too;
Human hearts and looks deceive me:—
 Thou art not, like them, untrue.
And while thou shalt smile upon me,
 God of wisdom, love, and might,
Foes may hate and friends may shun me,
 Show thy face and all is bright.

3.

O, NOW I see the crimson wave,
 The fountain deep and wide;
Jesus, my Lord, mighty to save,
 Points to his wounded side.

Cho.—The cleansing stream, I see, I see!
 I plunge, and O, it cleanseth me;
O, praise the Lord, it cleanseth me!
 It cleanseth me, yes, cleanseth me!

I see the new creation rise,
 I hear the speaking blood;
It speaks! polluted nature dies!
 Sinks 'neath the cleansing flood.

I rise to walk in heaven's own light,
 Above the world and sin,
With heart made pure, and garments white,
 And Christ enthroned within.

4.

I WILL sing you a song of that beautiful
  land,
 The far away home of the soul,
Where no storms ever beat on the glittering
  strand,
 While the years of eternity roll.

O, that home of my soul! in my visions and
  dreams,
 Its bright jasper wall I can see,
Till I fancy but thinly the veil intervenes,
 Between the fair city and me.

O, how sweet it will be in that beautiful
  land,
 So free from all sorrow or pain,
With songs on our lips, and with harps in
  our hands,
 To meet one another again.

5.

TO the cross of Christ, my Saviour,
 I had brought my weary soul,
Burdened, faint, and broken-hearted,
Praying: "Jesus make me whole."

Cho.—Glory, glory be to Jesus,
 I am counting all but dross,
I have found a full salvation,
 I am resting at the cross.

At the Cross, while prostrate lying,
 Jesus' blood flowed o'er my soul,
All my guilt and sin were covered,
 And he whispered "Child be whole."

At the Cross, I'm calmly trusting,
 Every moment now is sweet:
I am tasting of his glory,
 I am resting at his feet.

6.

I AM coming to the cross,
 I am poor, and weak, and blind;
I am counting all but dross,
 I shall full salvation find.

Cho.—I am trusting, Lord in thee; Blessed
  Lamb of Calvary;
 Humbly at thy cross I bow; Jesus
  saves me—saves me now.

Here I give up all to thee,—
 Friends, and time, and earthly store;
Soul and body thine to be—
 Wholly thine—forever more.

In the promises I trust;
 Now I feel the blood applied;
I am prostrate in the dust;
 I with Christ am crucified.

7.

WHO, who are those beside the chilly
  wave,
Just on the borders of the silent grave,
Shouting Jesus' power to save,
 "Washed in the blood of the Lamb?"

Cho.—"Sweeping thro' the gates" of the
  New Jerusalem,
 "Washed in the blood of the Lamb."

These, these are they who, in affliction's
  woes,
Ever have found in Jesus calm repose,
Such as from a pure heart flows,
 "Washed in the blood of the Lamb."

Safe, safe upon the ever shining shore,
Sin, pain, and death, and sorrow, all are o'er;
Happy now and evermore,
 "Washed in the blood of the Lamb."

1.

O FATHER, let me bear the cross;
  Make it my daily food,
Though with it thou dost send the loss
Of every earthly good.
Cho.—I am clinging to the cross,
  Yes, I'm clinging, clinging to the cross,
  I am clinging to the cross,
  Yes, I'm clinging, clinging to the cross.

Take house and lands and earthly fame;
  To all I am resign'd;
But let me make one earnest claim;
  Leave, leave the cross behind.

I know it costs me many tears;
  But they are tears of bliss,
And moments there outweigh the years
  Of selfish happiness.

2.

ONE more day's work for Jesus;
  One less of life for me!
But heav'n is nearer
And Christ is dearer
  Than yesterday to me;
His love and light
Fill all my soul to-night.
Ref.—One more day's work for Jesus,
  One more day's work for Jesus,
  One more day's work for Jesus,
  One less of life for me.

One more day's work for Jesus;
  Yes, and a weary day;
But heav'n shines clearer
And rest comes nearer
  At each step of the way;
And Christ is all,—
Before his face I fall.

3.

SIMPLY trusting every day,
  Trusting thro' a stormy way;
Even when my faith is small,
Trusting Jesus, that is all.
Cho.—Trusting him while life shall last,
  Trusting him till earth is past,
  Till within the jasper wall—
  Trusting Jesus, that is all.

Brightly doth his Spirit shine
Into this poor heart of mine;
While he leads, I cannot fall,
Trusting Jesus, that is all.

Trusting as the moments fly,
Trusting as the days go by,
Trusting him, whate'er befall—
Trusting Jesus, that is all.

4.

ON thee my heart is resting;
  Ah! this is rest indeed!
What else, Almighty Saviour,
  Can a poor sinner need?
Thy light is all my wisdom,
  Thy love is all my stay;
Our Father's home in glory,
  Draws nearer every day.

Great is my guilt, but greater
  The mercy thou dost give;
Thyself, a spotless offering,
  Hast died that I should live.
With thee my soul unfettered
  Has risen from the dust;
Thy blood is all my treasure;
  Thy word is all my trust.

Through me, thou gentle master,
  Thy purposes fulfill;
I yield myself forever
  To thy most holy will.
'Tis thou hast made me happy;
  'Tis thou hast set me free;
To whom shall I give glory
  For ever but to thee!

5.

COME to Jesus, come to Jesus,
  Come to Jesus just now,
Just now come to Jesus,
  Come to Jesus just now.

He will save you, etc.
He is able, etc.
He is willing, etc.
He is waiting, etc.
He will hear you, etc.
He will cleanse you, etc.
He'll renew you, etc.
He'll forgive you, etc.
If you trust him, etc.
He will save you, etc.

6.

HOW sweet the name of Jesus sounds
  In a believer's ear!
It soothes his sorrows, heals his wounds,
  And drives away his fear.
Cho.—Help me, dear Saviour, thee to own,
  And ever faithful be;
  And when thou sittest on thy throne,
  Dear Lord, remember me.

It makes the wounded spirit whole,
  And calms the troubled breast;
'Tis manna to the hungry soul,
  And for the weary, rest.

By thee my prayers acceptance gain,
  Although with sin defiled;
Satan accuses me in vain,
  And I am owned a child.

7.

COME, every soul by sin oppressed,
  There's mercy with the Lord,
And he will surely give you rest,
  By trusting in his word.
Cho.—Only trust him, only trust him,
  Only trust him now;
  He will save you, he will save you,
  He will save you now.

For Jesus shed his precious blood
  Rich blessings to bestow;
Plunge now into the crimson tide
  That washes white as snow.

Yes Jesus is the Truth, the Way,
  That leads you into rest;
Believe in him without delay,
  And you are fully blest.

9.

TO God—the Father, Son,
  And Spirit—Three in One,
All praise be given!
Crown him in every song;
To him your hearts belong;
Let all his praise prolong—
  On earth, in heaven.

1.

THERE are songs of joy that I loved to sing,
When my heart was as blithe as a bird in spring;
But the song I have learn'd is so full of cheer,
That the dawn shines out in the darkness drear.

Cho.—O, the new, new song, O, the new, new song,
I can sing it now with the ransom'd throng,
Power and dominion to him that shall reign;
Glory and praise to the Lamb that was slain.

There are strains of home that are as dear as life,
And I list to them oft 'mid the din of strife;
But I know of a home that is wondrous fair,
And I sing the psalm they are singing there.

I shall catch the gleam of its jasper wall,
When I come to the gloom of the even-fall,
For I know that the shadows, dreary and dim,
Have a path of light that will lead to him.
From "Gems of Praise."

2.

MY soul, be on thy guard,
Ten thousand foes arise;
The hosts of sin are pressing hard,
To draw thee from the skies.

Cho.—We're marching to Zion,
The beautiful city of God.

Oh, watch, and fight, and pray,
The battle ne'er give o'er;
Renew it boldly every day,
And help divine implore.

Ne'er think the vict'ry won,
Nor once at ease sit down;
Thy arduous work will not be done,
Till thou hast got thy crown.

Fight on, my soul, till death
Shall bring thee to thy God;
He'll take thee at thy parting breath,
Up to his blest abode.

3.

I SAT alone with life's memories
In sight of the crystal sea;
And I saw the thrones of the star-crowned ones,
With never a crown for me.
And there the voice of the Judge said, "Come,"
Of the Judge on the great white throne;
And I saw the star-crowned take their seats,
But none could I call my own.

I thought me then of my childhood days
The prayer at my mother's knee—
Of the counsels grave that my father gave,
The wrath I was warned to flee;
I said, "Is it then too late, too late?
Shut without must I stand for aye?"
And the Judge, will he say, "I know you not,"
Howe'er I may knock and pray?

I thought, I thought of the days of God,
I'd wasted in folly and sin—
Of the times I'd mocked when the Saviour knock'd,
And I would not let him in.
I thought, I thought of the vows I'd made
When I lay at death's dark door—
"Would he spare my life, I'd give up the strife,
And serve him forevermore."

I seemed as though I woke from a dream
How sweet was the light of day!
Melodious sounded the Sabbath bells
From towers that were far away.
I then became as a little child,
And I wept, and wept afresh;
For the Lord had taken my heart of stone
And given a heart of flesh.

Still oft I sit with life's memories,
And think of the crystal sea;
And I see the thrones of the star-crowned ones;
I know there's a crown for me.
And when the voice of the Judge says "Come,"
Of the Judge on the great white throne—
I know 'mid the thrones of the star-crowned ones,
There's one I shall call my own.

4.

'MID the deep and billowy ocean,
Raging now in wild commotion,
All secure, I'm ever singing,
For to Christ my soul is clinging,
Safe amid the tempest's shock,
Resting on the solid rock.

Cho.—On the Rock, on the Rock,
Resting safely on the Rock:
On the Rock, the solid Rock,
Resting safely on the Rock.

What though winds are howling 'round me?
What though darkness now surround me
Threatening utter desolation,
Christ the Rock is my salvation!
Calm amid the wildest shock,
On the everlasting Rock.

With my Saviour, what can harm me?
All hell's legions can't alarm me.
Jesus' mighty arms enclosing,
Sweetly is my soul reposing,
Safe amid the fiercest shock,
On the ever-blessed Rock.

5.

THERE is a gate that stands ajar,
And through its portals gleaming,
A radiance from the cross afar,
The Saviour's love revealing.

Ref.—Oh, depth of mercy! can it be
That gate was left ajar for me?
For me, for me?
Was left ajar for me?

That gate ajar stands free for all
Who seek through it salvation;
The rich and poor, the great and small,
Of every tribe and nation.

Press onward then, though foes may frown,
While mercy's gate is open;
Accept the cross, and win the crown,
Love's everlasting token.

Beyond the river's brink we'll lay
The cross that here is given,
And bear the crown of life away,
And love him more in heaven.

1.

THE world is overcome
By the blood of the Lamb.
My sins are washed away
In the blood of the Lamb.
I've washed my garments white
In the blood of the Lamb.
I soon shall gain the skies
Through the blood of the Lamb.

2.

HEAVENLY Father, bless me now;
At the cross of Christ I bow;
Take my guilt and grief away,
Hear and heal me now, I pray.

Ref.—Bless me now, bless me now,
Heavenly Father, bless me now!

Now, O Lord! this very hour,
Send thy grace and show thy power;
While I rest upon thy word:
Come and bless me now, O Lord!

Now, just now, for Jesus' sake,
Lift the clouds, the fetters break;
While I look, and as I cry,
Touch and cleanse me ere I die.

3.

THE precious blood of Jesus,
It washes white as snow.
My Saviour, I believe it,
For thou hast made me clean.
Shout, shout the victory,
We're on our journey home.
We'll wear a crown of glory
With Jesus in the sky.

4.

I BRING my sins to thee,
The sins I cannot count,
That all may cleansed be
In thy once open'd fount.

Cho.—Jesus paid it all
All to him I owe,
Sin had left a crimson stain,
He washes white as snow.

My heart to thee I bring,
The heart I cannot read,
A faithless wand'ring thing,
An evil heart indeed.

My life I bring to thee,
I would not be my own;
O Lord, let me be thine,
Be ever thine alone.

5.

GUIDE me, O thou great Jehovah,
Pilgrim through this barren land;
I am weak, but thou art mighty,
Hold me with thy powerful hand:
Bread of heaven, Bread of heaven,
Feed me till I want no more.

Open now the crystal fountain,
Whence the healing waters flow;
Let the fiery, cloudy pillar,
Lead me all my journey through:
Strong Deliverer, Strong Deliverer,
Be thou still my strength and shield.

6.

LORD, I approach the mercy-seat,
Where thou dost answer prayer;
There humbly fall before thy feet,
For none can perish there.

Cho.—I can, and I will, and I do believe
That Jesus died for me.

Thy promise is my only plea;
With this I venture nigh:
Thou callest burdened souls to thee,
And such, O Lord, am I.

O, wondrous love!—to bleed and die,
To bear the cross and shame,
That guilty sinners, such as I,
Might plead thy gracious name.

7.

WELCOME, welcome, dear Redeemer,
Welcome to this heart of mine;
Lord, I make a full surrender,
Every power and thought be thine;
Thine entirely,
Through eternal ages thine.

8.

HO! my comrades see the signal
Jesus waves on high!
Satan's battlements are reeling,
Hear our Captain's cry:

Cho.—"Storm the fort! for I am leading,
I have shown you how;"
Shout the answer back to heaven—
We are ready—*now!*

See! the lofty walls are frowning,
Held by Satan's power;
Sin enshrouds the world in darkness,
Now's the storming hour.

See! the prophets now are showing
How the fort must fall!
There is no such thing as failing,
Shout, my comrades, all!

Fierce and long the siege has lasted,
But the end is near:
Onward leads our great Commander,
Cheer! my comrades, cheer!

9.

'TIS religion that can give
Sweetest pleasures while we live;
'Tis religion must supply
Solid comfort when we die.

After death its joys will be
Lasting as eternity
Be the living God my friend,
Then my bliss shall never end.

10.

PRAISE God from whom all blessings flow,
Praise him, all creatures here below,
Praise him above, ye heavenly host,
Praise Father, Son and Holy Ghost.

INDEX.

Title	Page
ABUNDANTLY able to save,	4
A charge to keep I have,	91
Alas! and did my Saviour bleed?,	87
Albion C. M. D.,	94
All glory to the bleeding Lamb,	102
All hail the power of Jesus' name,	87
Am I a soldier of the cross,	87
And can I yet delay?,	91
Are you washed in the blood?,	15
Arise, my soul, arise,	95
Arlington C. M.,	86
At evening time it shall be light,	74
Avon, C. M.,	86
Awake, my soul, in joyful lays,	85
BADEA, S. M.,	90
Bartimeus, 8, 7,	98
Behold a stranger at the door,	104
Behold the throne of grace,	91
Blessed Jesus, thou art mine,	97
By thy birth and by thy tears,	106
CHEMUNG, L. M.,	82
Children of the heavenly king,	93
Christmas, C. M.,	88
Christ's Cross,	73
Come, every soul by sin oppressed,	108
Come, Holy Ghost, in love,	97
Come, Holy Spirit, calm my mind,	85
Come, Holy Spirit, heavenly dove,	89
Come, my fond fluttering heart,	95
Come, my Redeemer, come,	103
Come, my soul, thy suit prepare,	93
Come, Saviour, Jesus, from above,	83
Come, thou fount of every blessing,	99
Come to Jesus,	63
Come to Jesus just now,	108
Come to the Cross,	33
Come, ye sinners, poor and needy,	90
Come, ye that love the Lord,	91
Coming to Jesus,	32
Coronation C. M.,	86
Cressey, C. M.,	86
DEAR Father, to thy mercy-seat,	87
Dear Jesus, I long to be perfectly whole,	105
Death and eternity,	80
Decide to-night,	47
Deliverance will come,	64
Depth of mercy! can there be?,	93
Devotion L. M.	84
Did Christ o'er sinners weep?,	91
Down at the Cross,	70
Doxology, C. M.,	89
Doxology 8, 7, 4,	110
Doxology, L. M.,	110
Doxology, 7 6 1,	100
Doxology 8, 7,	95
Doxology, 6 4,	106
Doxology, 7, 6,	104
Draw me closer to thee,	42
Duke St. L. M.,	83
Dundee C. M.,	86
Durell 7,	92
EMMONS C. M.,	88
Enough for me,	72
Evangel 6, 4,	96
Evergreen Plain,	14
FAIRMOUNT S. M.,	99
Father, I stretch my hands to thee,	80
Forest L. M.,	84
Forever here my rest shall be,	87
For what are you waiting?,	18
From every stormy wind that blows,	85
GEBHARDT, 7,	92
God is coming,	25
Good news comes o'er the sea,	36
Guide me, O thou great Jehovah,	110
HALLELUJAH! he redeemed me,	29
Hamline, 8, 7,	94
Haste, O sinner, to be wise,	93
Hast thou heard of Jesus?,	45
Have you not a word for Jesus?,	42
Heavenly Father, bless me now,	110
He leadeth me,	102
He saves to the uttermost,	31
Hiding in the rock,	13
His keeping power,	39
Ho! my comrades, see the signal,	110
Horton, 7,	92
How sweet the name of Jesus sounds,	108
How tedious and tasteless the hours,	106
Hursley, L. M.,	84
I AM coming to the Cross,	107
I am listening,	50
I am thine own, O Christ,	104
I bring my sins to thee,	110
If thou leadest me,	26
I gave my life for thee,	103
I have a Saviour, he's pleading in glory,	100
I have entered the valley of blessing,	100
I know not if the dark or bright,	100
I lay my sins on Jesus,	101
I left it all with Jesus,	101
I love to tell the story,	101
I love the name of Jesus,	72
I'm but a stranger here,	105
In some way or other the Lord will provide,	101
Into thy hands, O Lord,	73
In the Christian's home in glory,	102
In the Cross of Christ I glory,	99
I shall be satisfied,	67
I shall be whiter than snow,	70
Is my name written there?,	27
I sat alone with life's memories,	109
I stand all bewildered with wonder,	104
I thirst, thou wounded Lamb of God,	85
I will sing you a song of that beautiful land,	107
I will trust my Redeemer,	7
I would not live without thee,	44
JESUS, and shall it ever be?,	85
Jesus, a word, a look from thee,	86
Jesus, I my cross have taken,	107
Jesus is passing this way,	52
Jesus, lead the way,	77
Jesus, let thy pitying eye,	106
Jesus, love me still,	48
Jesus, lover of my soul,	93
Jesus saves me every day,	105
Jesus, thine all-victorious love,	89
Just as I am, without one plea,	83
KNOCKING at the door,	34
LEAD me to Jesus,	10
Lenox, H. M.,	94
Lisbon, S. M.,	90
Lord, dismiss us with thy blessing,	99
Lord, I am thine, entirely thine,	85
Lord, I approach the mercy-seat,	110
Lord, I hear of showers of blessing,	108
Lord, we come before thee now,	93
Love divine, all love excelling,	95
Luton L. M.,	82

INDEX CONTINUED.

MARTYN, 7 D., ... 92
   Maytown, 8, 7, 4, ... 93
Mear, C. M. 88
Melody, C. M. 88
My anchor is holding, ... 55
My body, soul and spirit, ...106
My faith looks up to thee, ... 97
My Father's house, ... 64
My heavenly home is bright and fair, ...105
My hope is built on nothing less, ...104
My precious Bible, ... 30
My Redeemer lives, ... 87
My soul be on thy guard, ...109
My spirit is free, ... 43
'Mid the deep and billowy ocean, ...109

NEARER, my God, to thee, ... 97
   Nearer to me, ... 80
Nearer the Cross, ... 59
'Neath Elim's cooling palms, ... 57
Nettleton, 8, 7, 4, ... 98
No, not despairingly, ... 66
Nothing but the blood of Jesus, ... 78
No time for Jesus, ... 65
Now the solemn shadows darken, ... 99

O, Beulah land, ... 85
  O, bliss of the purified, ...100
O, come and dwell in me, ... 91
O Father, let me bear the cross, ...108
O God, forgive the years and years, ... 83
Oh, for a closer walk with God, ... 89
Oh, for a faith that will not shrink, ... 89
Oh, for a heart to praise my God, ... 89
Oh, for a thousand tongues to sing, ... 89
Oh, leave me not alone, ... 60
Oh, that I could repent, ... 91
O Jesus, delight of my soul!, ...104
O Lord, thy sovereign aid impart, ... 85
One more day's work for Jesus, ...108
Only waiting, ... 38
O, now I see the crimson wave, ...107
On thee my heart is resting, ...108
O, Paradise!, ... 95
Orie, L. M., ... 84
O, take me as I am, ... 74
O, take my fevered hands in thine, ... 83
O, that my load of sin were gone, ... 83
O, thou God of my salvation, ... 99
O, thou to whose all-searching sight, .. 85
O, to be nothing, ...104
Our sins on Christ were laid, ... 91

PEACE, 6, 4, ... 96
  Persuaded, ... 76
Pleyel's Hymn, 7, ... 92
Pray without ceasing, ... 54
Precious name, ... 8
Precious promise God hath given, ...101
Precious Saviour, thou dost save me, .105

RETURN and come to God, ... 91
  Return, O wanderer, return, ... 87
Rock of Ages, 7, 6 l, ... 96
Rock of Ages, cleft for me, ... 97
Room for Jesus, ... 81
Rosefield, 7, 6 l, ... 96

SAFE in Jesus, ... 51
  Satisfied, ... 66
Saviour, like a shepherd lead us, ...100
Say sinner, hath a voice within?, ... 85
Seeking for me, ... 41
Send me thy blessing, ... 35
Seymour, 7, ... 92
Shirland, S. M., ... 90
Show pity, Lord, O Lord forgive, ... 83
Sicilian Hymn, 8, 7, ... 98
Sienza, 6, 5, ... 96
Simply trusting every day, ...108
Sowing the seed by the daylight fair, .102

Stand up, stand up for Jesus, ... 99
St. Bernard, C. M., ... 88
Stocking, S. M., ... 90
St. Thomas, S. M., ... 90
Sweet hour of prayer, ...104
Sweet rivers of redeeming love, ... 95
Sweet the moments, rich in blessing, . 95

TAKE my life, and let it be, ... 97
  Talking with Jesus, ... 24
Tenderly lead me, ... 68
Tenney, C. H. M., ... 94
Tell me the old, old story, ...102
That open door, ... 22
The better day coming on, ... 81
The Cross and Crown, ... 19
The Lord is my light, ... 6
The mistakes of my life have been many,107
The precious blood of Jesus, ...110
The precious Lamb, ... 17
The prodigal coming home, ... 20
There are songs of joy, ...109
There is a fountain filled with blood, .106
There is a gate, ...109
There is a land of pure delight, ... 89
There is a spot to me more dear, ...105
There is joy in heaven, ... 46
There is life for a look, ...103
There's a highway for the ransomed, .101
There's a wideness in God's mercy, ...100
There's light over there, ... 62
There were ninety and nine, ...102
'Tis religion that can give, ...110
The Saviour's call, ... 12
The shadow of the Cross, ... 8
The shining city, ... 56
The sinner's friend, ... 75
The Sun of righteousness, ... 42
The wanderer's prayer, ... 16
The way, the truth, the life, ... 53
The world is overcome, ...110
This fountain cleanses from all sin, ... 79
This I did for thee, ... 76
This is why I love my Jesus, ... 9
Thou shepherd of Israel and mine, ... 95
To-day the Saviour calls, ...103
Tolling up the way, ... 5
To the Cross of Christ my Saviour, ...107
Touch and cleanse me, ... 21
Trusting in the promise, ... 40

VAIN man, thy fond pursuits forbear, .. 87

WAITING at the Cross, ... 23
  Warwick, C. M., ... 86
We are singing, ... 69
We are waiting, blessed Lord, ... 93
Webb, 7, 6, ... 98
We praise thee, O God, ...103
We speak of the realms of the blest, .101
What a friend we have in Jesus!, ...103
What means this eager anxious throng,106
When all thy mercies, O my God, ... 87
When I can read my title clear, ... 87
When I survey the wondrous cross, ... 83
When shall we meet again?, ... 97
When this song of praise shall cease, . 93
When we all get home, ... 53
Who, who are these beside the chilly wave,107
Why don't you come to Jesus?, ... 11
Why don't you receive him?, ... 74
Willie, 8, ... 94
Windham, L. M., ... 82
With tearful eyes I look around, ... 83
Wonderful grace, ... 61
Work before reward, ... 28

YET there is room, ...105
  Yield not to temptation, ...105

www.ingramcontent.com/pod-product-compliance
Lightning Source LLC
Chambersburg PA
CBHW031403160426
43196CB00007B/881